Discover Your Next
Mission from God

Julie Onderko

Discover Your Next Mission from God

⌒

Saints Who Found God's Will — and How You Can Too

SOPHIA INSTITUTE PRESS
Manchester, New Hampshire

Sophia Institute Press
Box 5284, Manchester, NH 03108
1-800-888-9344

www.SophiaInstitute.com

Sophia Institute Press® is a registered trademark of Sophia Institute.

Library of Congress Cataloging-in-Publication Data

Names: Onderko, Julie.
Title: Discover your next mission from God : saints who found God's will and how you can too / Julie Onderko.
Description: Manchester, New Hampshire : Sophia Institute Press, 2015. | Includes bibliographical references.
Identifiers: LCCN 2015037996 | ISBN 9781622822614 (pbk. : alk. paper)
Subjects: LCSH: Vocation—Catholic Church. | Church work--Catholic Church. |
Catholic Church--Doctrines.
Classification: LCC BX1795.W67 O53 2015 | DDC 248.4—dc23 LC record available at http://lccn.loc.gov/2015037996

First printing

To the Holy Family:

To Saint Joseph, my spiritual father
I am so grateful to him, and I love him so much.

To our Blessed Mother, Mary, through whom
my consecration to her Son, Jesus,
has changed my life: I love her and
she is the best mom anyone could ever have.

And to our Lord, Jesus Christ, the God-Man
and the absolute love of my life:
because of Him, all things are possible.

Contents

Acknowledgments

Although my husband, Tom, never wrote a word of this book, it simply couldn't have happened without him. This is his book, too. His unwavering and often sacrificial support made it possible. Tom is a gift to me, and I thank God for putting him in my life.

What would I do without my spiritual director, Father Giles Dimock, O.P.? Father Giles provided the theological safety net required to ensure faithfulness to the teachings of the Catholic Church. His ability to get to the heart of any matter with clarity has been invaluable to me. I greatly appreciate the guidance I have received from this good and wise priest.

Close friends are family that you choose. Steve and Karen Timm are like my big brother and sister. Without Karen's belief and confident insistence that I write this book, it is likely that I would have procrastinated indefinitely. And I cannot thank Steve enough—an absolutely fantastic writer and the best wordsmith I know. He taught me so much.

How can I adequately thank my dear friend and prayer partner, Rahles Goodell? Every writer needs someone with a nose for finding mistakes, and that was definitely Rahlie. Not only that: she's really onboard with the mission that others benefit from the saints featured in these pages.

Father Theodore Lange was so very helpful with the chapter on Saint Joseph. Father Theo also supported my writing ministry with a blessing, "May Saint Joseph guard this labor of love." I am deeply touched.

There are also several friends who have supported me, and I thank God for them. They listened, made suggestions, and encouraged me. *And you know who you are!*

I am eternally grateful for the heavenly connections made while writing this book. It has been a real adventure getting to know these saints; they have become my spiritual family. What an incredible blessing it is to have friends and family in high places!

Discover Your Next
Mission from God

1

℘

Seek God's Will from This Point On

God has created me to do him some definite service;
he has committed some work to me which he has not
committed to another. I have my mission.

—Blessed John Henry Newman

The Question

What is the defining question of our lives? That all-important question is found in *The Catechism of the Catholic Church*: "Lord, what do *you* want me to do?" (CCC 2706, emphasis added).

For our entire lives, we've been conditioned to make decisions based on what *we* want, and it goes against our grain to relinquish control to anyone, even to God. It seems as if to do so would require us to give up our freedom. But the opposite is true: we are most free and most human when we are squarely in God's will.

Perhaps we have messed up God's plan for us. It could be that God had a certain job in mind for us that would use our abilities and talents to further His kingdom on earth, but we did other things. Maybe we ignored God altogether and lived a self-centered sinful life. It's possible that God had religious life in mind for us, but we didn't listen and got married instead. We could be on course, slightly off course, or way off the mark.

Even if we are not on course, no worries! Think of a Global Positioning System (GPS). If we do not follow the instructions, the GPS continually recalibrates to lead us to our destination. It does not send us back to the beginning to start all over. We don't travel the roads that we have passed up. Rather, the GPS sends us to our destination *from where we currently stand.* That is how it is with God, but infinitely better.

God can redeem our past. It is quite mysterious how He can take any terrible thing and make something far more beautiful out of it than we ever could have imagined. Think of the fall of mankind in the Garden of Eden. Now that appeared to be a horrible derailment of God's plan, yet when God restored the human family, we found ourselves far better off than our first parents. We get to *be* in the Body of Christ; we get to share in the family of God by a radical change in our nature that actually divinizes us. We might not see it in our earthly lifetimes, and we might not understand it, but when we give our past sins, mistakes, and regrets to God and follow His will, He will take care of all those regrets.

We exist in this challenging day and time for a reason. From all eternity, God had our particular circumstances in mind for our arrival on this earth. And He made sure we would have the help we need.

Works of Mercy

It is human nature to get excited about something new, such as discovering our next mission from God. But any good thing can get out of balance, displacing what we ought to be doing. Pope John Paul II warned about "the temptation of being so strongly

interested in Church services and tasks that some fail to become
actively engaged in their responsibilities in the professional, social,
cultural and political world."[1] In discerning our mission, there is
the danger of becoming self-absorbed. But if we do it God's way,
He will reveal His will for us, even as we focus on others.

God requires certain things of each and every one of us; in
fact, we can't get into Heaven without them. These requirements
are an indispensable part of the journey that leads to our mission:

> Before him will be gathered all the nations, and he will sepa-
> rate them one from another as a shepherd separates the sheep
> from the goats, and he will place the sheep at his right hand,
> but the goats at the left. Then the King will say to those at
> his right hand, "Come, O blessed of my Father, inherit the
> kingdom prepared for you from the foundation of the world;
> for I was hungry and you gave me food, I was thirsty and you
> gave me drink, I was a stranger and you welcomed me, I was
> naked and you clothed me, I was sick and you visited me, I
> was in prison and you came to me." (Matt 25:32–36)

What happens to the goats on the left? Jesus tells them:

"Depart from me, you cursed, into the eternal fire prepared
for the devil and his angels; for I was hungry and you gave me
no food, I was thirsty and you gave me no drink, I was a stranger
and you did not welcome me, naked and you did not clothe me,
sick and in prison and you did not visit me." Then they also
will answer, "Lord, when did we see thee hungry or thirsty or a
stranger or naked or sick or in prison, and did not minister to
thee?" Then he will answer them, "Truly, I say to you, as you did

---

[1] John Paul II, post-synodal apostolic exhortation *Christifideles
Laici*, Rome, December 30, 1988, no. 2.

it not to one of the least of these, you did it not to me." And they will go away into eternal punishment, but the righteous into eternal life." (Matt. 25:41–46).

It is essential to our salvation that we minister to the Lord through those in need. So, while we are discerning, praying, investigating, and searching for our mission, we might as well get going on the Corporal and Spiritual Works of Mercy. Regardless of our forthcoming mission, we need to do them, and it is often in the *doing* that we discern our mission.

The Corporal Works of Mercy, which tend to physical needs, are:

- to feed the hungry
- to give drink to the thirsty
- to clothe the naked
- to shelter the homeless
- to visit the sick and imprisoned
- to ransom the captive
- to bury the dead

The Spiritual Works of Mercy, which tend to spiritual and emotional needs, are:

- to instruct the ignorant
- to counsel the doubtful
- to admonish the sinner
- to bear wrongs patiently
- to forgive offences willingly
- to comfort the afflicted
- to pray for the living and the dead

Seek God's Will from This Point On

It can be overwhelming to see all the works of mercy listed, but they are quite manageable when we consider them in light of our circumstances. For example, God does not expect the father of a family to leave his wife and children to work as a missionary in a third-world country, but perhaps he could teach a religious-education course at his parish. A mother who has young children at home may not be able to leave them or take them with her to serve at a homeless shelter, but she might take her children to visit a lonely neighbor.

There are works of mercy that complement our state in life, whether we are rich or poor, whether we have lots of time or very little, whether we enjoy good health or are infirm. When it comes to the Corporal and Spiritual Works of Mercy, there's something—and plenty of it—for everybody. Turning our attention away from ourselves and toward others will enable us to see opportunities to do works of mercy that we never noticed before.

Help Along the Way

As well as opportunities to serve Him, God gives us help to do so. We each have a close companion and guide, a guardian angel, to assist us on our earthly sojourn. The saints certainly availed themselves of the help of their angels. Saint Francis de Sales advised:

> Make friends with the angels, who though invisible are always with you. Often invoke them, constantly praise them, and make good use of their help and assistance in all your temporal and spiritual affairs.[2]

---

[2] Saint Francis de Sales, *Introduction to the Devout Life* (Charlotte, NC: TAN Books, 1994), pt. 2, chap. 16.

Our Lord Jesus, in His great generosity, also gave us His Mother. It doesn't get any better than having the same mom as Jesus.

> Then he said to the disciple, "Behold, your mother!" And from that hour the disciple took her to his own home. (John 19:27)

Who better than our Blessed Mother can help us as we discern God's specific plans in our lives? She went through the process; she had to ponder and pray; and she did not know the whole story when she gave her fiat to the Lord.

We've already been given some incredible help: our Blessed Mother and our guardian angels. But there's more! Our elder brothers and sisters in Christ, the saints, want to help us find our missions and carry them out. And they have incredible stories, insights, and advice to share.

Our Response

We could not be in a better place or time than right where we are now. This may be difficult to believe, but remember, although our perspective is limited, God's view is eternal. He has a plan, and we need to figure out how to cooperate with Him in that plan.

Given this understanding, what is our response? Will we allow the expectations of others to write the story of our life? Or, will we seek God's will and carry it out?

We are often fearful of the very things that will bring us peace and courage. It doesn't make sense to fear God's will for us. Echoing Jesus' words, Saint John Paul II told us: "Be not afraid!"[3]

---

[3] Pope St. John Paul II, Homily of His Holiness John Paul II for the Inauguration of His Pontificate, October 22, 1979.

Seek God's Will from This Point On

Relinquishing the power to control our lives and giving it to the One who knows us better than we know ourselves, the One who has all the answers, the One who is most capable, makes perfect sense. Our abandonment to God's purpose, and the required trust in Him and His plan, is where our fulfillment, our greatest desire, is found. It is the only answer that will satisfy.

Reflection

Blessed John Henry Newman considered the ultimate question: "Lord, what do You want me to do?" The cardinal shares his wisdom and insights as we ask the same question and begin our journey.

> I am created to do something or to be something for which no one else is created. I have a place in God's counsels, in God's world, which no one else has. Whether I be rich or poor, despised or esteemed by man, God knows me and calls me by my name.[4]
>
> God has created me to do him some definite service; he has committed some work to me which he has not committed to another. I have my mission — I may never know it in this life, but I shall be told it in the next. Somehow I am necessary for his purposes, as necessary in my place as an archangel in his — if, indeed, I fail, God can raise another, as he could make the stones children of Abraham. Yet I have a part in this great work; I am a link in a chain, a bond of connection between persons. He has not created me for naught.

[4] John Henry Newman, *Prayers, Verses, and Devotions* (San Francisco: Ignatius Press, 1989), 338.

I shall do good. I shall do his work. I shall be an angel of peace, a preacher of truth in my own place, though not intending it, if I do but keep his commandments and serve him in my calling.

Therefore I will trust him. Whatever, wherever I am, I can never be thrown away. If I am in sickness, my sickness may serve him; in perplexity, my perplexity may serve him; if I am in sorrow, my sorrow may serve him. My sickness, or perplexity, or sorrow may be necessary causes of some great end, which is quite beyond us. He does nothing in vain. He may prolong my life; he may shorten it. He knows what he is about. He may take away my friends. He may throw me among strangers. He may make me feel desolate, make my spirits sink, hide the future from me — still he knows what he is about.[5]

---

[5] John Henry Newman, *Everyday Meditations* (Manchester, NH: Sophia Institute Press, 2013), 7, 120.

2

⪗

Employ Guidance and Direction

*We should not trust every word we hear or every feeling in our
hearts; rather, we should bring such matters before God and care-
fully ponder them at our leisure. . . . Instead of following your own
notions, consult someone who is wise and conscientious, and seek
to be guided by one who is better than you.*

—Thomas à Kempis, *The Imitation of Christ*

Spiritual Direction

Something special happens when we sincerely seek God's will.
The answers frequently come through our normal activities. An
off-hand comment by a stranger might specifically address what
we have been considering. We may find a burning desire in our
hearts that persists, compelling us to give it our full consideration.
It is often through ordinary things — a book, a situation, or a
coincidence — that God speaks to us. However, those weightier
directives that we believe are from God ought to be properly
evaluated through wise spiritual counsel. Pope Emeritus Benedict
XVI tells us:

As she has never failed to do, again today the Church continues to recommend the practice of spiritual direction,

not only to all those who wish to follow the Lord closely, but to every Christian who wishes to live responsibly his baptism, that is, the new life in Christ. Everyone, in fact, and in a particular way all those who have received the divine call to a closer following, needs to be supported personally by a sure guide in doctrine and expert in the things of God.[6]

Avoiding the Dangers

Saint Faustina Kowalska gave us tremendous advice concerning spiritual direction as a means of discerning our ideas, inclinations, and inspirations. She told us not to trust ourselves. Sister Faustina, who was a mystic and accustomed to frequent visits from Jesus, and less frequent visits from her guardian angel and the Blessed Mother, did not trust herself. When Jesus told her something, in a sense, she doubted His words until they were confirmed, usually through her spiritual director. In her diary, she explains:

> Still, a soul which is faithful to God cannot confirm its own inspirations; it must submit them to the control of a very wise and learned priest; and until it is quite certain, it should remain distrustful. It should not, on its own initiative alone, put its trust in these inspirations and all other higher graces, because it can thus expose itself to great losses.
>
> Even though a soul may immediately distinguish between false inspirations and those of God, it should

---

[6] Pope Benedict XVI, Papal address to the Teresianum, *Zenit*, May 11, 2011, accessed June 23, 2015, http://www.zenit.org/en/articles/papal-address-to-the-teresianum.

nevertheless be careful, because many things are uncertain. *God is pleased and rejoices when a soul distrusts Him for His own sake*; because it loves Him, it is prudent and itself asks and searches for help to make certain that it is really God who is acting within it. And once a well-instructed confessor has confirmed this, the soul should be at peace and give itself up to God, according to His directions; that is, according to the directions of the confessor.[7]

Faustina is right. Even with the best of intentions, we can be tricked or misguided. Saint Paul warns us about the devil's deceptions: "for even Satan disguises himself as an angel of light. So it is not strange if his servants also disguise themselves as servants of righteousness" (2 Cor. 11:14–15).

It would be ideal if we could all have a holy, prudent, and insightful spiritual director. Certainly, any spiritual director should be loyal and obedient to the Church, as well as devoted to the Blessed Mother. A priest would be an optimal spiritual director, since he could also be our confessor. Members of religious orders and qualified laypersons, however, can also impart wise counsel.

We might ask a priest, a religious, or someone with an impeccable reputation for holiness, wisdom, and loyalty to the Church if he or she could meet with us regularly, perhaps once a month. Sometimes the answer will be no, and we must continue to pray, search, and ask. Other times, after a meeting or two, we will realize that the person is not a good fit for us. Although finding the right spiritual director is often time consuming, it is definitely

[7] Sister Maria Faustina Kowalska, *Diary: Divine Mercy in My Soul* (Stockbridge, MA: Marians of the Immaculate Conception, 2000), no. 139.

worthwhile. We should persevere even though it may take longer than we like. Saint Faustina said:

> Oh, how great a grace it is to have a spiritual director! One makes more rapid progress in virtue, sees the will of God more clearly, fulfills it more faithfully, and follows a road that is sure and free of dangers. The director knows how to avoid the rocks against which the souls could be shattered.[8]

Saint Catherine of Siena, who received messages from God the Father (recorded in *The Dialogue*) and personal visits from Jesus, did not counsel herself. Blessed Raymond of Capua, O.P., was her confessor, spiritual director, and closest friend. Like most people who have made substantial progress in the spiritual life (the saints), Catherine did not go it alone, and neither should we.

It's not always possible to connect with a good spiritual director. Certainly we should pray about it and continue investigating. Lacking a spiritual director is not a reason to put our spiritual growth on hold, however. We must still seek God's will in our lives. If God wants us to have a spiritual director, we will have one — in His time. Meanwhile, let's not overlook the wise counsel He has provided.

Holy Friendship

We have only to look at the lives of the saints to see many holy friendships. These relationships are numerous throughout Church history — Monica and Augustine; Ignatius of Loyola and Francis Xavier; Francis of Assisi and Clare; Teresa of Ávila and John of the Cross; and Francis de Sales and Jane de Chantal, to

---

[8] *Diary*, no. 139.

name only a few. Pope John Paul II enjoyed relationships with his spiritual contemporaries, such as Mother Teresa, Padre Pio of Pietrelcina (one brief encounter when the pope was a young man and by letter in later years), and Fulton Sheen.

People walking the road to holiness frequently seek others on the same path. When we ponder the fruit produced by such relationships, it is simply stunning. Looking back on her life, Saint Teresa of Ávila realized that, at times, she could have used a good friend:

> A great evil it is for a soul to be alone in the midst of so many dangers. It seems to me that if I should have had someone to talk all this over with, it would have helped me.[9]

She therefore recommends the right kinds of friendship:

> For this reason I would counsel those who practice prayer to seek, at least in the beginning, friendship and association with other persons having the same interest. This is something most important even though the association may be only to help one another with prayers.[10]

Saint Teresa explains further, contrasting the difference between human attachments and authentic Christian friendship:

> I don't know why it is not permitted that persons beginning truly to love and serve God, talk with some others about their joys and trials, which all who practice prayer undergo. For if the friendship they desire to have with

[9] Teresa of Ávila, *The Book of Her Life*, trans. Kieran Kavanaugh, O.C.D., and Otilio Rodriguez, O.C.D. (Indianapolis: Hackett, 2008), 40.
[10] Ibid.

His Majesty [God] is authentic, there is no reason to fear vainglory.[11]

The path to holiness, to fulfilling God's intentions for our lives, in all likelihood, includes friends. Saint Francis de Sales tells us, "For those who live in the world and desire to embrace true virtue, it is necessary to unite together in holy, sacred friendship."[12]

In these relationships, all parties (it could be a group) should sincerely seek God's will for the others. Individuals should not gather to promote their own agendas or self-serving intentions. Saint Paul tells us how to be an authentic friend, "Let no one seek his own good, but the good of his neighbor" (1 Cor. 10:24).

Our companions on the spiritual journey, those who truly love us and want the best for us, will speak the truth with love. When it is called for, we can expect gentle and firm corrections from them as well as support during trials. They will help us to stay on track and avoid sin.

When it comes to making decisions and discerning God's will, these spiritual allies will intercede to God for us. They will be available as conduits of His love and guidance in our decisions, in our joys, and in our challenges.

In our friendships in Christ, Jesus is the catalyst and the bond. It is amazing how quickly a deep friendship can grow if it is rooted in the Lord. This begins with prayer, asking God to provide those people He selects to be our companions. He often brings these friends into our lives *before* we ask. We might find them at a Bible study; a prayer group; a men's group, such as the Knights of Columbus; a women's group, such as the Altar

---

[11] Teresa of Ávila, *The Book of Her Life*, 40.

[12] Fr. Joseph Esper, *Saintly Solutions to Life's Common Problems* (Manchester, NH: Sophia Institute Press, 2001), 28.

Society; in line at the grocery store; or even in our own families. The possibilities are endless. If we have our spiritual antennae up, we will find them.

Spiritual Direction from Heaven

Recall the heavenly help that God offers us in discerning His will. As members of the Body of Christ, we have access to a relationship with the saints in Heaven.

We have already mentioned Mary, the Queen of Saints, as a heavenly guide. When we look at the saints who were spot-on when it came to discerning their mission from God and carrying it out, we find a commonality. They were all devoted to our Blessed Mother, and she helped them discern God's will and carry it out.

Have you ever thought of how awesome it would be to have a saint for a spiritual director—someone such as Ignatius of Loyola, Thérèse of Lisieux, or Maximilian Kolbe? In a way, we can. Many of the spiritual giants in the history of our Church have put their advice, lessons, and experiences in writing for us. This does not substitute for the interaction experienced with a spiritual director or our wise and holy friends, but the saints' wisdom and advice can contribute greatly to our discernment and our mission.

Saint Maximilian Kolbe and His Heavenly Benefactors

Saint Maximilian Kolbe had his spiritual directors. In his case, they were his superiors in the Franciscan Order. He realized that, by his obedience to them, he was doing the will of God. If the Virgin Mary, whom he affectionately called "Our Little Mother," wanted something done, she would see to it through the decisions of his supervisors.

Filled with zeal for saving souls, Kolbe established an evangelization center in the late 1920s near Warsaw, Poland, and called it Niepokalanów, "the City of the Immaculate." In just over a decade, Niepokalanów was the largest Catholic religious house in the world, using the most modern technology of the time to evangelize Poland.

When Father Kolbe approached his superiors to ask their permission to establish a mission friary like Niepokalanów in the Orient, they were understandably apprehensive. After all, Kolbe did not have a concrete plan, and he also suffered from tuberculosis. But he was a man of deep prayer and faith. His superiors must have also considered Kolbe's close relationship with Mary. Whatever he did at Mary's bidding, no matter how outlandish it sounded at first, repeatedly proved out. If they denied his request, there might be Heaven to answer to—after all, who would want to oppose the Blessed Mother's plans?

"Mary will see to it. It's her Son's business,"[13] is how Father Kolbe often answered those who doubted the enterprises he proposed. Although he did not speak Chinese or Japanese, did not know exactly where he and his four friars would end up, and had no connections in the Orient, he *did know* that the Blessed Mother wanted him to found a mission there. He confidently replied to his superiors' concerns, "The Blessed Mother has her plan ready."[14] They granted their permission but reminded Father Kolbe that they could offer no financial support for his venture. He assured them, "That's all right. I've got my benefactors lined up."[15]

---

[13] "St. Maximilian Mary Kolbe," EWTN, accessed July 17, 2015, https://www.ewtn.com/saintsHoly/saints/M/stmaximilian-marykolbe.asp.

[14] Patricia Treece, *A Man for Others: Maximilian Kolbe Saint of Auschwitz* (Huntington, IN: Our Sunday Visitor, 1982), 43.

[15] Ibid., 44.

Who were his benefactors? Saint Thérèse of Lisieux, Saint Bernadette of Lourdes, and Saint Joseph Cottolengo. Father Kolbe's relationship with these saints in Heaven was as real as any friendship he experienced on earth. Recognizing that this mission was a team effort orchestrated within the Communion of Saints, Kolbe made a short pilgrimage to honor each saint before leaving for the Orient.

After arriving in Japan with no connections, penniless, and not knowing the language, Kolbe and his friars successfully established the Japanese mission on the outskirts of Nagasaki. Although hardship and sacrifice were required of these four Franciscans, it was obvious that there was additional (tangible and intangible) assistance from the three heavenly benefactors.

Why these three particular saints? There are undoubtedly many reasons for Maximilian's relationship with these souls regarding the mission to Japan. Let's consider the most obvious.

Although Saint Thérèse of Lisieux was a cloistered Carmelite nun who never left her convent, she had the heart of a missionary. It is through her intercession that many missions receive the assistance they need. She is in fact one of the patron saints of the missions. However, years earlier, when Maximilian was still a seminarian, he and Thérèse made a deal: he would pray for her canonization (she would be canonized in 1925) if she would advocate for his militia, whose members would engage in the spiritual battle for souls.[16]

During an apparition, young Bernadette of Lourdes, France, asked the Blessed Mother (not knowing the beautiful lady's identity), "Would you be so kind as to tell me who you are?" The answer: "I am the Immaculate Conception." Kolbe himself

---

[16] Ibid.

spent his life pondering this reality. Bernadette and Maximilian shared a special love for and devotion to the Blessed Mother. Father Kolbe's work, the print apostolate, and the monasteries that functioned as evangelization centers were all dedicated to Mary under her title of the Immaculate Conception.

The involvement of the third heavenly benefactor, Saint Joseph Cottolengo, was less obvious. Joseph Cottolengo was known for his care of the poor. Of course, Kolbe and his friars were always helpful and generous to those in need, but their primary focus was the print apostolate for the purpose of evangelization.

It was not until after Maximilian Kolbe's martyrdom at Auschwitz that we more clearly see Cottolengo's connection with the Japanese mission. The atomic bomb dropped on Nagasaki in 1945 destroyed everything in the mission's immediate vicinity, but the monastery was miraculously preserved. The friars, too, were virtually unscathed, receiving only minor injuries. The Franciscans in charge of the mission were able to house hundreds of children who had suddenly found themselves orphaned.[17] This response perfectly reflects the attitude of Joseph Cottolengo, who relied daily on divine providence in the care of those in desperate need. He certainly belonged in the trio of Kolbe's saintly benefactors.

⌒

Reflection

When we finally get to Heaven, hopefully we will have already established a divine connection, an eventful history, with some of the saints there. That's how it is with the Communion of Saints. We have friends in high places. These magnanimous souls

---

[17] Treece, A Man for Others, 51.

will be waiting for us, and we in turn will be able to thank them in person for their holy friendship. Saint Francis de Sales tells us:

> If the bond of communion is love, devotion, and Christian perfection, then your friendship will be precious indeed: precious because it has its origin in God, because it is maintained in God, and because it will endure forever in Him.[18]

[18] Paul Thigpen, A *Dictionary of Quotes from the Saints* (Ann Arbor: Chairs Books, Servant Publications, 2001), 94.

3

⌒

Utilize the Past — Your Life Is Your Formation

Father, I am seeking: I am hesitant and uncertain, but will you,
O God, watch over each step of mine and guide me.

—Saint Augustine

Sudanese Slave Child: Saint Josephine Bakhita

At times we might face events or circumstances that make it
seem impossible to move forward in our lives. But a horrific event
or situation that we think is the end of the story ... simply *is not*.
The Lord will not be outdone by evil. No matter how people
exercise their free will to do malicious and wicked things to
others, God will bring good from it. Undeniable proof is found
in the life of Saint Josephine Bakhita.

In the dark of night, seven-year-old Bakhita and another
Sudanese girl were hiding under some large plants. They had run
away from the slave market. Treated inhumanely and having witnessed atrocities perpetrated on other captives, these two little
girls were immersed in a nightmare from which they would not
awaken. The children had traveled for days, chained together
for much of the journey. They talked, telling each other about
their families and wondering if they would ever see them again.

When their chains had been temporarily removed and the slave trader's back was turned, they had fled into the night. Their captors never found them, but someone else did. Trusting this man who told them he would help them find their parents, the two children once again found themselves in chains.[19]

We do not know how or to what extent the temporary escape changed the trajectory of Bakhita's life. But the particular circumstances that would lead her to God had been set in motion. On that night on the run, when Bakhita was just seven years old, a mystical experience would place a certainty deep within her heart: a message of providence and of being watched after. Here is the story in the words of Sister Turco, a close friend of Bakhita:

> Bakhita once told me that something happened after she and her companion escaped from their owner, on the very first night they spent in the forest. While everything was dark all around them and they were hiding under some plants, she suddenly saw a beautiful figure take shape in the sky. Surrounded by light, this figure was smiling at her and pointed out the way she should follow. Without telling anything about this to her companion, she confidently followed the direction that this mysterious figure indicated. In this way, she found the strength and courage to continue on, and thus they were saved from the wild beasts. Near dawn the figure disappeared, and she did not see it again.
>
> After many years, when she was a nun and sacristan, without even recalling the earlier occasion in the forest, one morning as she was opening the little door to the

---

[19] Roberto Italo Zanini, *Bakhita: From Slave to Saint* (San Francisco: Ignatius Press, 2013), 50–53.

rectory, she saw at her side a beautiful young man, radiant with light. Surprised, she stopped, then recognized him and remembered. She wanted to speak but felt as if her tongue had been nailed to the roof of her mouth, and her limbs became stiff. The young man smiled at her and then disappeared. "It must have been your guardian angel," I told her. "Yes, I believe it was too," she replied.[20]

Bakhita would be bought and sold five times in the slave markets of El Obeid and Khartoum. She was regularly whipped and beaten without cause. She was inflicted with a ritual scarring of her backside — a horrific ordeal that almost killed her. She would witness many atrocities perpetrated on other slaves. This inhumane treatment lasted six years until an Italian diplomat bought her and treated her kindly. Three years later (Bakhita was sixteen by this time), he brought her to Italy with him and gave her to his friend Agosto Michieli and his wife, Lady Turina. Bakhita became the nanny for the Michielis' little daughter, Mimmina.

Servant of the Lord

A friend of Michieli, Iluminato Checchini, took an interest in the spiritual formation of Bakhita. He gave the young slave woman a crucifix, and although she did not realize its significance, Bakhita was deeply touched. The Holy Spirit was working mysteriously in her soul:

> As he gave me the crucifix, he kissed it with devotion, then explained that Jesus Christ, the Son of God, had died for me. I did not know what a crucifix was, but I was moved by a mysterious power to keep it hidden, out

[20] Ibid., 53–54.

of fear that the lady [Turina] would take it away. I had never hidden anything before, because I had never been attached to anything. I remember that I looked at it in secret and felt something inside that I could not explain.[21]

The Michielis intended to relocate permanently to Africa. In preparation for their final move, they traveled there to get things in order. They decided it best not to bring their little daughter on that preliminary trip. Due to the influence of Iluminato Checchini, the couple arranged boarding with the Canossian Sisters in Venice for Mimmina and her nanny, Bakhita.

It was from the Canossian Sisters that Bakhita received her first catechetical instructions. Although she had no previous exposure to Christianity, this "African flower"[22] knew about Almighty God (the *Paron,* she called Him) in the most basic way, in that His existence is written on every human heart.

From childhood I had felt [God] in my heart without knowing who he was. I remember [in her village in Africa] looking at the moon and stars and the beautiful things in nature and saying to myself, "Who could be the Master of these beautiful things?" And I experienced a great desire to see him, to know him and honor him.[23]

From her catechist, Sister Marietta Fabretti, we get a glimpse of Bakhita's yearning to learn about God:

---

[21] Zanini, *Bakhita,* 79.

[22] "Josephine Bakhita (1869–1947)," Vatican website, accessed, July 10, 2015, http://www.vatican.va/news_services/liturgy/saints/ns_lit_doc_20001001_giuseppina-bakhita_en.html.

[23] Zanini, *Bakhita,* 81.

When I asked her whether she truly wanted to know the Lord, she responded, "yes!" I was struck by the tremendous joy that was inside that Yes.[24]

About one year later, Lady Turina returned to Venice to get Mimmina and her Sudanese nanny for the final move to Africa. Bakhita politely but firmly refused to leave. Many legal avenues were tried by Lady Turina to force Bakhita to go with her. But slavery was illegal in Italy, and by this time, Bakhita was no longer a minor under the guardianship of the Michielis. The Italian authorities would not force Bakhita to go with Lady Turina.

Three-year-old Mimmina cried. The little girl had never known a life without her nanny. And Bakhita's heart was broken too; she loved Mimmina. But the young Sudanese woman was resolute. Deep in her soul, Bakhita realized what was at stake: "No, I will not leave the house of the Lord. It would mean my ruin."[25]

A Taste of Heaven on Earth

Bakhita remained with the Canossian Sisters. She was drawn to the suffering Christ and spent many hours in prayer before the crucifix. "Seek God alone and Christ crucified," were the instructions given to the Sisters by their foundress, Saint Magdalene of Canossa. Given Bakhita's identification with the Cross of Christ, it is no surprise that she was called to the religious life as a Canossian. Sister Josephine Bakhita joined the Canossian Daughters of Charity on the feast of the Immaculate Conception in 1896.

Sister Josephine Bakhita would lovingly embrace the different tasks assigned to her: cook, sacristan, and portress. During World War I, she nursed wounded soldiers. Bakhita could readily

---

[24] Ibid., 83.
[25] Ibid., 89.

identify with their agonies. The soldiers were separated from their families, in physical pain, and in some cases in danger of death. Like Bakhita, many had witnessed the lonely sufferings and deaths of their companions. But Bakhita was able to deliver the most needed spiritual medicine. According to one of the Sisters, "she showed the soldiers such tender care and attentiveness that she was able to comfort their very souls."[26]

Later in her life, Sister Bakhita was asked to share her personal story. This led to speaking engagements all over Italy to promote the missions—a task she was rather shy about since it drew attention to her. But she was successful in raising awareness for the needs of the missions, especially in Africa. Mother Bakhita would have loved to return to Africa as a missionary herself, but by this time she was getting older. Her health would not be up to the rigors of this demanding work.

It was during her travels around Italy to propagate the missions that she arranged to meet another Sudanese nun in the cloister of the Visitation Sisters of Soresina. Imagine what it must have been like for these two women (now both in their sixties) to share their stories—which were so similar. After piecing their histories together, they discovered that they were sisters! Two years before Bakhita's abduction, her older sister had been kidnapped and never found, and this Visitation Sister, Maria Agnostina, *was she*. She too had gone through the slave markets and had been ransomed by an Italian. Sister Maria had been entrusted to the care of the Salesians, which had led to her conversion and decision to enter religious life.

Bakhita's traveling companion, Sister Benetti, describes the emotional meeting between the two Sudanese nuns:

[26] Zanini, *Bakhita*, 105.

The brief but joyful meeting between the little brown Visitation sister and the little brown Canossian nun was indescribable. Words cannot convey how much happiness dear Sister Maria Agostina felt in seeing good Mother Bakhita as her own dearest sister. She was completely convinced of this, and it seemed to me that Bakhita was too.... Sister Agostina, filled with joy and emotion, said, "Oh, how I thank the Lord for giving me this satisfaction," and her tears came streaming down. Bakhita replied, "We will see each other again."[27]

Sister Josephine Bakhita was extremely grateful for the privilege of being Catholic. When passing the baptismal font, she would reverently kiss it and exclaim, "Here, I became a daughter of God!"[28] This simple woman was described as "pure as an angel" and "meek as a lamb."[29] She was joyfully aware of God's companionship in her life. When speaking about His constant loving presence, she said, "If I had known it when I was a slave, I would never have suffered so much."[30] Sister Josephine Bakhita kept her eyes on the goal of Heaven. She continually shared this simple truth with those she met: "Take heart, then: let us work, suffer, pray, and become saints, for this is the one thing necessary."[31]

Whether we have been victimized by others, willingly participated in evil, or been both victim and perpetrator, our history is

---

[27] Ibid., 115–116.

[28] Brian O'Neel, *39 New Saints You Should Know* (Cincinnati: Servant Books, 2010), 52.

[29] Ann Ball, *Modern Saints, Book Two* (Rockford, IL: TAN Books, 1990), 442.

[30] Ibid., 441.

[31] Zanini, *Bakhita*, 77.

part of our formation. No matter what has happened, we need not despair. In fact, we can be assured that God will orchestrate everything for His plan. Saint Paul clarifies this for us: "We know that all things work together for good for those who love God, who are called according to his purpose" (Rom. 8:28).

A Soldier Is Prepared: Saint Ignatius of Loyola

A career military soldier for early sixteenth-century Spain, Ignatius of Loyola would be forever impacted by his defending the Citadel of Pamplona. During this battle with the French, he was struck by a cannon ball, which badly broke one of his legs and injured the other. When he went down, his garrison surrendered.

Ignatius was admired and respected not only by his men, but also by his French victors. French field doctors nursed him for about two weeks and then transported him by stretcher (a ten-day trip across rugged terrain) to one of his family's holdings, a castle at Loyola.

During his convalescence, which lasted almost a year, Ignatius suffered a great deal. His leg required rebreaking and resetting two more times—all without anesthesia. The third "butchery," as he called it, was done for vain reasons:

> One bone below the knee remained on top of another, shortening his leg. The bone protruded ... an ugly sight. He was unable to abide it because he was determined to follow the world and he thought that it would deform him.[32]

---

[32] Ignatius wrote his autobiography in the third person and refers to himself in this quotation. *The Autobiography of St. Ignatius Loyola*, trans. Joseph O'Callaghan (New York: Harper Torchbooks, 1974), 22.

Ignatius wasn't exaggerating about his vanity, worldliness, and pride. During all three surgeries, one on the battlefield and two at the castle, "he never spoke a word nor showed any sign of pain other than to clench his fists."[33]

These details are important to consider if we are to grasp the drastic change that was required of Ignatius when he gave his fidelity wholeheartedly to God. This quality of single-mindedness, his ambitious nature, and his tenacity—when channeled in God's direction—would impact the world for centuries to come.

After enduring these excruciating procedures, a razor-thin brush with death, and futile efforts to stretch his leg, he was left with a permanent limp. Ignatius had always been an active man, fully engaged in all his endeavors. Extravagant about his dress and the quest for glory, he admits to self-gratifying pursuits.

> He was a man given over to vanities of the world; with great and vain desire to win fame he delighted especially in the exercise of arms.[34]

To be confined to a bed, totally dependent on others, must have been the worst of the torments he endured. That he would have preferred the chivalrous romantic novels of his day to pass the time and distract his mind is an understatement. Oh, for a good diversion! But only two books were to be found in the castle of Loyola during his recovery: one on the life of Christ and another on the saints. These two books he read many times, resulting in a complete and total conversion.

What if a huge library of novels had been available to Ignatius? What would have happened then? The two supplied books

---

[33] Ibid., 22.
[34] Ibid., 21.

were absolutely pivotal to his conversion — and there was nothing else competing for his attention. We can see how important it is to have good materials available to us. Moreover, there are priceless benefits to removing those distractions that lead us away from God.

Ignatius left the castle of Loyola a changed man. During those endless hours of recovery, he had discerned, through prayer, study, and using his imagination, that he would become a soldier of the Catholic Faith.

A Focus on Following God's Will

Picture a classroom full of young boys. Ignatius is sitting among them. He isn't the instructor. He is one of the students. They are all learning Latin together.

At thirty-seven years of age, Ignatius "was found to be deficient in fundamentals."[35] If he were to become a priest, it was imperative that he learn Latin. He was penniless and begged for the food he ate but somehow managed to acquire the necessary education, even when it obliged him to go back to primary school. Nothing would stop Ignatius from following God's will, not even the most humbling of circumstances.

It's a good thing that Ignatius didn't think, "Well, all I know is soldiering. I'm in my thirties now [comparable to being in one's fifties today], and it's too late to start all over in life. I'm not healthy. I've got a very bad limp and stomach troubles." There were many legitimate reasons Ignatius might have questioned the path God had chosen for him. But here again we see the intensity with which he was known to have focused on his pursuits: only now, he was pursuing God.

---

[35] *The Autobiography of St. Ignatius Loyola*, 73.

Equipped with Our Experiences

Ignatius used his military experience and leadership skills to establish the Society of Jesus, and he applied those lessons to the disciplines he developed for his order. For instance, his advice to "divide and conquer," in our struggle against sin is derived from his background as a soldier and commander.

All of our experiences can be placed in the service of the Lord: our mistakes, our careers, our relationships — everything. Our personal histories, no matter how sheltered or colorful, contribute to our formation. The very thing we think disqualifies us might be exactly what *uniquely* qualifies us for our mission. For example, pro-life workers have in their ranks women who have had abortions themselves. These women have had a change of heart and want to help others avoid the mistakes they made. From personal experience, they can say to someone considering an abortion, "I *know* how you feel now, and I also know what it's like to live with that regret."

God doesn't need our perfection, our planning, our money, or our talents. Our Lord doesn't *need* anything, but in His great humility, He requests our yes, our fiat, to His plans for us. The circumstances and experiences that lead to our yes are as individual as we are.

Ignatius's temperament, his personality traits, his experiences, his physical abilities and inabilities all, in some way, contributed to his God-given mission. It's the same for us. Our life *is* our formation.

Reflection

Ignatius's total surrender to the Lord and the specific plan God had for him led to the establishment of the Society of Jesus: the Jesuits. At its core is the foundational directive given by

Ignatius: the First Principle and Foundation. This directive not only demonstrates Ignatius's radical abandonment to the will of God but also serves as a filter, removing those things that should be rejected as we discern God's plans in our lives.

The First Principle and Foundation of the Jesuits
Man is created to praise, reverence, and serve God our Lord, and by this means to save his soul.

And the other things on the face of the earth are created for man to help him in attaining the end for which he is created.

Hence, man is to make use of them in as far as they help him in the attainment of his end, and he must rid himself of them in as far as they prove a hindrance to him.

Therefore, we must make ourselves indifferent to all created things, as far as we are allowed free choice and are not under any prohibition. Consequently, as far as we are concerned, we should not prefer health to sickness, riches to poverty, honor to dishonor, a long life to a short life. The same holds for all other things.

Our one desire and choice should be what is more conducive to the end for which we are created.[36]

---

[36] John A. Hardon, ed., *The Treasury of Catholic Wisdom* (San Francisco: Ignatius Press, 1987), 388; see also "Ignatian Spirituality," Social Justice and Ecology Secretariat, accessed September 29, 2015, http://www.sjweb.info/sjs/pjold/pj_show.cfm?PubTextID=760.

4

⁀

Practice Humility, the Essential Ingredient

Think of God in terms of faith, of your neighbor in terms of charity, and of yourself in terms of humility. Rate yourself low. Speak of God with veneration, speak of your neighbor as you would wish him to speak of you, and speak of yourself humbly, or not at all.

—St. John Bosco

An Unseen Foe

Approaching the altar rail at Saint Francis Xavier Church to receive Communion during an early-morning Sunday Mass, Matt Talbot, a young Irish laborer, was unexpectedly inundated with a crushing sense of dread and discouragement. Overwhelmed with depression, he became physically ill and was compelled to leave before receiving the Blessed Sacrament. When outside the church, the physical illness with its oppressive mood evaporated.

Matt Talbot wandered the streets of Dublin, Ireland, on that day in 1884 in a bit of a daze, not sure what to make of his experience. About an hour later, he found himself in front of another Catholic Church and went in for Mass. All was well until it was time to receive the Blessed Sacrament. The previous feelings returned with increased intensity, and he was physically driven from the church—again without receiving Holy Communion. Once outdoors, wellness returned.

Matt continued to walk the streets for an hour or so, befuddled but determined. It was still early, and there were other opportunities to attend Sunday Mass. When the episode occurred a third time, Matt recognized the experience for the spiritual battle that it was.

He returned to Saint Francis Xavier Church. Without care of who might be watching or what others thought of him, Matt threw himself face down on the church steps, extending his arms in the form of a cross, and cried, "Surely, O Lord, I am not going to fall again into the habits I have left!" He prayed passionately, imploring the help of the Virgin Mary. After about ten minutes, he got up and walked into the church to attend the next Mass. And this time, he *did* receive our Lord in the Blessed Sacrament and never encountered this struggle again.[37] Humility had beaten the devil: it always does.

Saint Vincent de Paul tells us:

> The most powerful weapon to conquer the devil is humility. For as he does not know at all how to employ it, neither does he know how to defend himself from it.[38]

Matt Talbot's Addiction

Persons who have successfully overcome serious addictions will say that they could not have conquered it on their own: they needed help. Folks with any manner of obsessions (food, alcohol, drugs, pornography, shopping, and so forth) who have

---

[37] Sir Joseph A. Glynn, *The Life of Matt Talbot*, 4th ed. (Dublin: Truth Society of Ireland, 1942), chap. 2, "His Conversion."

[38] Esper, *Saintly Solutions*, 261.

time after time tried and failed to break free of the destructive habits will admit (if they are honest) that on some level, they attempted to tackle their obsessions on their own. Matt Talbot was desperate that day when he repeatedly tried to receive Communion at Mass. It had been only a few weeks since he had taken the pledge to give up drinking—an enormous struggle that he could not manage by himself. Matt *knew* how much he needed our Lord in the Blessed Sacrament if he were to remain sober. If he missed this personal encounter with the Lord, he most likely would be too weak to resist the temptation to drink.

A daily drunk—that is what Matt had been for sixteen years of his life. And he had started young, at twelve years of age, when he went to work as a messenger boy for a wine seller. Even though he was intoxicated most of the time, Matt was surprisingly a good worker and could keep a job. All his money, and then some (he would run up debts he could not pay), was spent at the pub. So, hopeless at times, Matt was known to sell his boots or clothes so he could buy another drink. Given his lifestyle, he could not afford to support himself, so he lived with his mother. The poor woman never received any monetary support from her son, and during those sixteen years of his drunkenness, she never saw him sober.

Taking the Pledge

The decisive moment came when Matt was out of money, and his friends would not take him drinking with them. They snubbed him, and it's no wonder, given his reputation: Matt could be an expensive friend. Unable to get the alcohol he desired, he began to sober up. It was then, in a moment of grace, that Matt made a decision. His sister Mary Andrews tells us what happened when he came home that day:

My mother said, "You're home early, Matt, and you're sober!" He replied, "Yes, Mother, I am." After dinner he remained in the house, which was not usual, and finally he remarked to my mother, "I'm going to take the pledge." She smiled and said, "Go, in God's name, but don't take it unless you are going to keep it." He said, "I'll go in God's name."

As he was going out Mother said, "God give you strength to keep it." He went to Clonliffe, made his confession, and took the pledge for three months. He had been a couple of years away from the sacraments then. Next morning — Sunday — he went to Holy Communion. On Monday he went to 5 a.m. Mass in Gardiner Street and was at his work as usual at 6 a.m. This he made a regular practice from that time on. But after his work, to keep away from his companions, he used to walk to a distant church … and remain there until bedtime. …

He had a bad time of it at first and sometimes said to my mother, that, when the three months were up, he would drink again.[39]

By the grace of God, Matt Talbot remained sober for the rest of his life.

Discerning God's Will
Turning to God repeatedly every day in order to break his addiction to alcohol had other spiritual benefits. Through prayer, fasting, daily Mass, and frequent Confession, this humble

---

[39] Bert Ghezzi, *Voices of the Saints: A Year of Readings* (New York: Doubleday, 2000), 514–515.

man—who realized he could accomplish nothing without God—grew exceedingly in holiness. Not trusting in his own perceptions and judgments, he prudently sought the assistance of a wise spiritual director. He joined the Third Order Franciscans, studied the lives of the saints, and was deeply devoted to the Blessed Mother.

Matt was not one to preach to others. He gave advice only when asked and sometimes not even then; but wanting to grow continually in virtue and holiness, he kept helpful notes. Here is one such note he wrote to himself.

> Three things I cannot escape: the eye of God, the voice of conscience, the stroke of death. In company guard your tongue. In your family guard your temper. When alone guard your thoughts.[40]

Being a devout Catholic of strong moral character and a reliable workman, Matt Talbot was considered good husband material. He had caught the eye of a pious Catholic girl who had observed him and realized he would make a fine husband. The young woman was a cook where he was employed, and she sought him out. First, she informed him that she had saved money, enough to furnish a home. She followed this information with a request that he pray a novena to determine if it was God's will that they should marry.

To our twenty-first-century sensibilities, this might seem an odd way to find a person to marry. By giving the idea an unbiased appraisal, however, we can legitimately see that it definitely has merit. The young woman saw that Matt was qualified, observed

---

[40] Ibid., 514–515.

his good character, and then, through her prayers and his, sought the will of God.

Seeing that she was intent on correctly discerning the decision, Matt took her suggestion seriously and prayed the novena. In doing so, he realized that he did not have a vocation to married life. He said the Blessed Mother had told him not to marry, and he never did.[41]

Walking in the Truth

Saint Teresa of Ávila put it simply and accurately when she stated, "Humility is walking in the truth."[42] "I could never be a saint" is something that we often hear or perhaps say ourselves. Even though it might sound humble, it is contrary to God's designs for us. God created us for sainthood; His will for us is that we become saints.

Shortly before she died, Saint Thérèse of Lisieux said, "I feel that my mission is going to begin, my mission to cause the Good Lord to be loved as I love Him ... to give my little way to souls. I WANT TO SPEND MY HEAVEN DOING GOOD ON EARTH."[43] Her words convey confidence in her sanctity. She implies that she is going to Heaven, and there she will receive her next mission from God. On the surface, it sounds a little prideful. After all, who would make a statement like that when they are dying?

Honest and humble saints would.

---

[41] Glynn, *The Life of Matt Talbot*, chap. 3, "Growing in Holiness."

[42] Saint Teresa of Ávila, *The Interior Castle*, trans. John Dalton (London: Aeterna Press, 2015), 122.

[43] Thérèse of Lisieux, *The Story of a Soul*, in *The Complete Thérèse*, ed. and trans. Robert Edmonson (Brewster, MA: Paraclete Press, 2009), 261.

Practice Humility, the Essential Ingredient

Bride of Christ: Saint Catherine of Siena

Thirteenth-century Italians didn't always know what to make of the fiery young Catherine from Siena. She came from a respectable family, and her devotion to our Lord was above reproach. Even so, she certainly did not behave as expected for a woman of her day.

During this often-turbulent time in Italian history, alliances created through marriage were necessary to maintain a family's wealth and solvency. Be that as it may, Catherine had taken a vow of virginity; she would have only Jesus for a husband. She refused the marriage arranged by her family, which upset them a great deal.

In time, her father, Giacomo, realized there was something very special going on with his determined daughter. He therefore allowed Catherine the privacy of her own room, where she remained in seclusion for three years, leaving only for brief periods to get a bite of food or attend Mass. This was her formation period. By the end of it, Catherine had attained the most intimate of all unions with Christ: the mystical marriage. When Christ took Catherine as His spouse, he told her:

> From this time forward, daughter, act firmly and decisively in everything that in my Providence I shall ask you to do. Armed as you are with the strength of faith, you will overcome all your enemies and be happy.[44]

If her family and neighbors already thought her eccentric, they would continue to be amazed and sometimes shocked after she emerged from her hermit-like existence in the Benincasa

---

[44] Raymond of Capua, *The Life of St. Catherine of Siena by her Confessor* (Charlotte, NC: TAN Books, 2011), 82.

home. Catherine's life was consumed with one unique mission after another.

Any young single woman who had taken a vow of virginity would have been expected to enter the convent, but Catherine could not be confined behind convent walls if she were to carry out God's will in her life. Rather, she became a Dominican tertiary; all the other Third-Order Dominicans were widows, Catherine being the exception. And, of course, people talked. "What does she want to go traipsing about for? She is a woman! If she wants to serve God, why doesn't she stay at home?"[45]

Catherine is probably most famous for convincing Pope Gregory to return to Rome after popes had resided for seventy-four years in Avignon, France. Unmarried thirteenth-century women didn't go around telling the pope, bishops, or government leaders what they should do. But at the Lord's request, the obedient Catherine courageously delivered His messages.

She denied herself comforts and pleasures, slept on a board, and practiced continual mortifications. When the plague swept through Siena, Catherine nursed the afflicted and buried the dead while working with only a few hours of sleep for days at a time.

Many miracles are attributed to this saint's intervention. Catherine multiplied food and wine, cured the sick, and even raised the dead. She is one of the few saints who received the stigmata. She did not want others to know about it, however, so she begged the Lord to make it invisible, which He did.

This mystic saint experienced visits from Jesus, the Virgin Mary, and Saint Dominic. Her only book, *The Dialogue*, comprises messages she received directly from God the Father. She

---

[45] Raymond of Capua, *The Life of St. Catherine of Siena*, 305.

was often found in a state of spiritual ecstasy after receiving Holy Communion. During these experiences of intimate union with Christ, Catherine's body was unresponsive, and there was no stimulation that could rouse her.

When a Humble Soul Asks

When Catherine's mother, Lapa, died after disregarding the state of her soul, and without the sacrament of Confession, Catherine fell before Jesus and cried:

> Lord my God, are these the promises you made to me, that none of my house should go to hell?... Now I find that she [Lapa] has died without the sacraments of the Church. By your infinite mercy I beg you not to let me be defrauded like this. As long as there is life in my body I shall not move from here until you have restored my mother to me alive.[46]

If there was one motivation that Catherine shared passionately with Jesus, it was a desire for the salvation of souls. On the surface, her petition doesn't sound like a humble prayer, but when we understand the context, Catherine's response exemplifies true humility. There was not a bit of selfishness in her request. Being separated from her mother in this life wasn't Catherine's motivation at all. It was, instead, concern for the loss of her mother's eternal soul. Her impassioned response: "As long as there is life in my body I shall not move from here until you have restored my mother to me alive," is like saying, "I would rather die than have this soul lost." This attitude of Catherine's is completely consistent with the motivations of her Bridegroom, Jesus Christ,

[46] Ibid., 196–197.

who *did* die to save us. Raymond of Capua, Catherine's spiritual director gave us this explanation:

> After delaying Lapa's death for a long time, He [the Lord] suddenly permitted her to die without confession, in order to show how much merit the holy virgin [Catherine] had in His eyes.[47]

And Raymond continues by telling us how this story ended:

> The virgin prayed, and the cries of her heart ascended to highest heaven: all her grief, united with her humble, copious tears, rose up before the eyes of the Most High; and then it was impossible that she should not be heard. And in fact the Lord of all comfort and mercy did hear her. Before the eyes of the three women present, Lapa's body suddenly began to move; her soul was restored and she again made the movements of a living person.[48]

Humility, the Great Weapon against Evil

We have an intelligent and crafty enemy in Satan and all his demons. Masters of human behavior, these evildoers know how to trip us up. Our only recourse is total reliance on God: in other words — humility.

In fact, it was Catherine's humility that continually confounded the devil. One occasion concerned an eight-year-old girl, Lorenza, who was possessed by a demon. At first Catherine avoided the girl and her parents, saying, "Alas! Every day I am tormented by evil spirits. Do you think I want anybody else's?" But when, out

---

[47] Raymond of Capua, *The Life of St. Catherine of Siena*, 196.
[48] Ibid., 197.

of obedience to her spiritual director, she was obliged to stay with the child, Catherine went into spiritual battle on the girl's behalf.

Today, it is often assumed that historical, even biblical, accounts of demonic possessions were in reality cases of mental illness. In this situation we can be assured of the accuracy. This little girl was possessed by an extremely obstinate demon. Catherine's spiritual director, Raymond of Capua, was personally involved, knew the parents of the girl, and testified to the events:

> It was discovered that the evil spirit that was plaguing her [Lorenza] was in the habit of speaking a very elegant form of Latin through her mouth, despite the fact that the child knew nothing about the language, and could solve deep and difficult problems and reveal the sins and state of conscience of particular individuals.[49]

The little girl was freed from the evil spirit after spending one night with Catherine. Since previous efforts had failed, Raymond of Capua questioned Catherine about it:

> After a long struggle, realizing that he [the evil spirit] would be forced to leave Lorenza, he said, "If I come out of here I will enter into you." Immediately the virgin [Catherine] replied, "If the Lord wills it so, and I know that without His permission you can do nothing, God forbid that I should prevent you, or in any other way alienate myself from His Will or set myself up against Him." Whereupon the proud spirit, struck amidships by such humility, lost nearly all the power he had over the little girl.[50]

[49] Ibid., 217.
[50] Ibid., 221.

For most of us, dealing with the devil is not so straightforward or discernible. Instead, the evil enemy tempts us to pride in two rather sly but common ways. The first entices us to a false sense of humility, which is really pride incognito. It goes something like this: *You could never be a saint; you are too weak. How could God use you? Come on, who do you think you are anyway?*

With the other approach the devil tries to ensnare us by appealing directly to our self-importance: *You are pretty special. See what you did? You know better than they do. Who are they to tell you what to do?* But if we humble ourselves, as Catherine *always did*, we will not be confused.

The devil would first appeal to a false sense of pride, telling Catherine she was wretched and couldn't possibly be worthy to do what God asked of her, and she would agree. But she immediately appealed to God for His mercy and help. Nothing is impossible with God. If He wanted to use her "wretched self" for His work, then, of course, she would cooperate.

When that ploy didn't work, the devil would appeal to her pride, pointing out all that had been done through her. There *were* a multitude of miracles as well as her influence in the Church and in politics, which were unprecedented accomplishments for a woman of her day. Catherine would again humble herself, acknowledging her nothingness and total dependency on God. She really frustrated the devil:

> Damnable woman! There is no getting at you! If I throw you down in confusion, you lift yourself up to mercy. If I exalt you, you throw yourself down.[51]

---

[51] Ralph Martin, *The Fulfillment of All Desire* (Steubenville, OH: Emmaus Road Publishing, 2006), 189.

Practice Humility, the Essential Ingredient

Humility is the moral virtue on which all the other virtues are built. It is the essential ingredient; without it we simply cannot progress in our spiritual life. Humility recognizes our total dependence on God and our creaturely equality with others. Saint Catherine of Siena tells us:

> You, Deep Well of Charity, it seems You are so madly in love with your creatures that You could not live without us. Yet You are our God and have no need of us. Your greatness is no greater for our wellbeing, nor are You harmed by any harm that comes to us. For You are Supreme Eternal Goodness. What could move You to such mercy? Neither duty nor any need You have of us, but only love.[52]

That truth, of course, includes the splendor of what God has created in the human person. While praying for the salvation of a sinner, Catherine was allowed to see how incredibly valuable, precious, and beautiful the human soul really is. She shared her experience with her spiritual director:

> [God] showed me the beauty of that soul ... Father [Raymond of Capua], if you could see the beauty of the rational soul, you would not doubt for a minute that you would be prepared to give your life a hundred times over for the salvation of that soul, for there is nothing in this world that can compare with such beauty.[53]

Humility is found in realizing that we can do nothing on our own. We are totally dependent on God. He is the Creator, and

---

[52] Catherine of Siena, *The Dialogue*, trans. Suzanne Noffke (New York: Paulist Press, 1980), 63.

[53] Raymond of Capua, *The Life of St. Catherine of Siena*, 119.

we are His creatures. None of us is more or less valuable than another. In addition to that bit of truth, we also find that we have an infinite value. We are all precious; we each possess a beautiful soul, and all of us are loved by God, individually and passionately. Therefore, everything we perceive, everything we do, and every thought we think ought to be put through the filter of these realities. According to Saint Teresa of Ávila, "There is more value in a little study of humility and in a single act of it than in all the knowledge in the world."

⮂

Reflection

If we are serious about discerning God's will and carrying out the missions He offers us, then we should pray for the grace to grow in the virtue of humility.

Litany of Humility[54]
O Jesus! meek and humble of heart, hear me.
From the desire of being esteemed, *deliver me, Jesus.*
From the desire of being loved, *deliver me, Jesus.*
From the desire of being extolled, *deliver me, Jesus.*
From the desire of being honored, *deliver me, Jesus.*
From the desire of being praised, *deliver me, Jesus.*
From the desire of being preferred to others, *deliver me, Jesus.*
From the desire of being consulted, *deliver me, Jesus.*
From the desire of being approved, *deliver me, Jesus.*

[54] By Rafael Cardinal Merry del Val (1865–1930), secretary of state for Pope Saint Pius X, https://www.ewtn.com/Devotionals/prayers/humility.htm.

Practice Humility, the Essential Ingredient

From the fear of being humiliated, *deliver me, Jesus.*
From the fear of being despised, *deliver me, Jesus.*
From the fear of suffering rebukes, *deliver me, Jesus.*
From the fear of being calumniated, *deliver me, Jesus.*
From the fear of being forgotten, *deliver me, Jesus.*
From the fear of being ridiculed, *deliver me, Jesus.*
From the fear of being wronged, *deliver me, Jesus.*
From the fear of being suspected, *deliver me, Jesus.*
That others may be loved more than I, *Jesus, grant me
    the grace to desire it.*
That others may be esteemed more than I, *Jesus, grant
    me the grace to desire it.*
That, in the opinion of the world, others may increase
    and I may decrease, *Jesus, grant me the grace to desire it.*
That others may be chosen and I set aside, *Jesus, grant me
    the grace to desire it.*
That others may be praised and I unnoticed, *Jesus, grant
    me the grace to desire it.*
That others may be preferred to me in everything, *Jesus,
    grant me the grace to desire it.*
That others may become holier than I, provided that
    I may become as holy as I should, *Jesus, grant me the
    grace to desire it.*

5

☞

Develop Your Personal Prayer Life

*Pray with great confidence, with confidence based upon the
goodness and infinite generosity of God and upon the promises
of Jesus Christ. God is a spring of living water which flows
unceasingly into the hearts of those who pray."*

—Saint Louis de Montfort, *The Secret of the Rosary*

Wife, Mother, and Physician: Saint Gianna Molla

Foundational to the saints' extraordinary witness is a commitment to the Lord in personal prayer. The saints' relationships with Jesus Christ were first in their lives. From that emerged their good works, their inspirations, and their heroic virtues. We see this in Saint Gianna Molla.

A quick glance at the life of Gianna Molla might leave us wondering, "How did she manage it all?" Gianna was a wife, a mother, a physician, a committed volunteer with the Saint Vincent de Paul Society, and a leader of the young women of Catholic Action. She had a knack for balance in life, which for her included recreation such as skiing and dancing. How could anyone manage so much and remain present to her patients, her husband, her children, the young women she mentored, and all the souls that came under her sphere of influence? There is only one answer: her source was Jesus Himself. He was an unending supply of joy, perseverance, and love that she continually radiated to those around her.

A principled woman, this contemporary saint is known for her unshakable decision to choose the life of her unborn child over her own. Early in her fourth pregnancy, a benign tumor was found growing on her uterine wall. The recommended surgery, which would pose the least risk to Gianna herself, would have aborted the baby—an option that Gianna and her husband rejected outright. Instead she requested a surgery that was considerably more risky for her: the removal of only the tumor.

After the delicate surgery, the pregnancy continued normally until few days before the due date, when it became apparent that the delivery would be difficult and possibly life threatening. It could come down to that dreaded choice: the life of the child or the life of the mother. If that became the case, Gianna put her child first and made her wishes known to her doctor. Gianna also required her husband to promise to choose the baby. "I insist," she said.[55]

Almost every mother's greatest fear is to lose a child. Next to that—to leave her children without their mother. Even though others can step in to care lovingly for the children, there is a tremendous loss; no other person can perfectly replace a child's mother. And when a mother of young children is facing the possibility of her death, her thoughts are for her children. She is keenly aware of their loss and its multiple repercussions. The thought of leaving her little ones behind is a torment of unimaginable proportions.

[55] Pietro Molla and Elio Guerriero, *Saint Gianna Molla: Wife, Mother, Doctor* (San Francisco: Ignatius Press, 2004), 9.

The quite-possible scenario that one or the other, but not both, could be saved was not to be. (What a blessing for Gianna's husband, Pietro: imagine the anguish he would face over such a choice!) Baby Gianna Emanuela was born on April 21, 1962. Her mother's decision early in the pregnancy to save her unborn baby by surgical means had led to Gianna Emanuela's live birth. However, that initial choice, which held such hope to save them both, turned out to be fatal for the mother. Gianna developed an infection, from which she died seven days after giving birth. The thirty-nine-year-old mother left behind her husband and four young children.

Discernment

Gianna had the advantage of a strong Italian Catholic upbringing. Being raised in a Catholic home, however, does not ensure sanctity. On our own, we each must respond to Christ's invitation. A turning point came for Gianna when she was just sixteen: she made an Ignatian retreat. Although up to this point she had been a faithful Catholic, this young woman deepened her relationship with Jesus by purposefully surrendering her entire life to Him. Gianna's work, her service to humanity, all her decisions, everything would be done for Jesus. This was the means by which she would achieve sainthood. She wrote:

> I make the holy resolution to do everything for Jesus. All my works, all my disappointments, I offer everything to Jesus.... I want to ask the Lord to help me not to go to hell.... I ask the Lord that he make me understand his great mercy.[56]

---

[56] Ibid., 27.

Prayer and meditation were indispensable to Gianna. Seeking God's will for her life, she wrote:

> What is a vocation? It is a gift from God—it comes from God Himself! Our concern, then, should be to know the will of God. We should enter onto the path that God wills for us, not by "forcing the door," but when God wills and as God wills.[57]

Believing that she was called to the vocation of marriage required great faith and patience on her part. She did not "force the door" by hurrying things along. Gianna waited on the Lord and did not marry until she was thirty-three. The marriage of Pietro and Gianna Molla, which was filled with love, respect, and abundant joy, would last only six years. And their sacramental union would produce their "treasures," as they called them: their four beautiful children.

Before her marriage, Gianna discerned a call to the healing ministry. She became a physician and worked as a general practitioner as well as a pediatrician. Her husband recalls her tenderness toward her patients:

> Dozens of times I saw her at work and could admire her delicacy, her attentions, her affection. It was a mother's affection, that of a woman who had enthusiastically embraced the vocations to motherhood and the medical profession.... She had a predilection for the elderly, whom she loved to visit at home, even without being called.[58]

---

[57] Molla and Guerriero, *Saint Gianna Molla*, 8.
[58] Ibid., 85, 72.

Develop Your Personal Prayer Life

Prayer and meditation were priorities for the young doctor, and this gave her greater insight into spiritual realities. Mentoring the young women of Catholic Action, she shared the source of her joy, strength, and love:

> When we make our Communion ... we are physically joined to Jesus Christ so that we may say with Saint Paul: "It is not I who live, but Christ who lives in me" (Gal 2:20).... Thus, our hearts are the living cenacles, the monstrances through whose glass the world ought to see Christ.[59]

These spiritual insights permeated everything Gianna did. She saw how her work as a physician was a "priestly mission."

> We have opportunities that a priest does not. Our mission is not ended when medicines are of no more use. There is the soul to take to God, and your word will have authority. Every physician should deliver a patient to the priest. These Catholic doctors, how necessary they are!
>
> The great mystery of man—he has a body but also a supernatural soul—is Jesus: "Whoever visits the sick, helps me." Priestly mission: as the priest can touch Jesus, so we touch Jesus in the bodies of our patients—poor, young, old, children.
>
> May Jesus be able to make himself seen through us; may he find many physicians who offer themselves for him: "When you have finished your profession—if you have done that—come to enjoy the life of God, because I was sick, and you healed me."[60]

---

[59] Ibid., 65–66.
[60] Ibid., 75.

Gianna continually refueled her soul as a daily communicant. She craved intimate visits with Jesus and made frequent visits to the Blessed Sacrament. All that Saint Gianna did was drawn out of her relationship with Jesus. She spent time with Him, seeking His will for her and then doing it. This is the way of sainthood.

The Hour That Formed His Life:
Venerable Fulton Sheen

When Fulton Sheen was ordained to the priesthood, he made a commitment "to spend a continuous Holy Hour every day in the presence of our Lord in the Blessed Sacrament."[61] There were three reasons for this. First, the Holy Hour shares in the work of redemption; it is "an hour of reparation to combat the hour of evil; an hour of victimal union with the Cross to overcome the anti-love of sin."[62] Second, it provides Jesus with the companionship that He did not receive from His friends during His agony in the garden (see Matt. 26:40). Third, the young Father Sheen wanted to be transformed more and more into the likeness of Jesus Christ:

> We become like that which we gaze upon. Looking into a sunset, the face takes on a golden glow. Looking at the Eucharistic Lord for an hour transforms the heart in a mysterious way as the face of Moses was transformed after his companionship with God on the mountain. Something happens to us similar to that which happened to the disciples at Emmaus.[63]

---

[61] Fulton J. Sheen, *Treasure in Clay* (Garden City: Doubleday, 1980), 187–199.
[62] Ibid.
[63] Ibid.

And, over time, Bishop Fulton Sheen was transformed. On one occasion, when he was in Africa for the Propagation of the Missions, he had medals to give out to five hundred lepers. The first man approached and extended his hand, which was not much more than a stub, the disease having eaten away his flesh. The bishop, feeling a natural repugnance to the rotted tissue, dropped the medal into what was left of the man's hand, but it slipped off and fell to the ground. The bishop immediately corrected himself, stooped down, picked up the medal, and by God's grace, gave it to the man—touching him. And Bishop Sheen passed out the 499 remaining medals, placing them directly in each leper's hand.[64]

When the newly ordained Father Sheen made the commitment to a daily Holy Hour, he had no way of knowing how indispensable it would be. His future would include becoming a worldwide television celebrity and traveling the globe where cheering mobs would throng to listen to him.

This daily Holy Hour was Sheen's "tether"[65] to the tabernacle and therefore to reality. How else could he, or anyone, have resisted all the trappings that becoming a global celebrity presented? Entering repeatedly into a personal encounter with Jesus kept his vision clear, putting things in proper order and anchoring him to his mission from God.

Even though Archbishop Fulton Sheen treasured the daily Holy Hour and encouraged its practice, he realized it wasn't for everybody.

I know thousands ... who have not had the practice of making frequent visits to the Blessed Sacrament, but I

---

[64] *Archbishop Fulton Sheen, Servant of All* (San Francisco: Ignatius Press, 2011), DVD.

[65] Sheen, *Treasure in Clay*, 187–199.

am absolutely sure that, in the sight of God, they are a thousand more times worthy than I.[66]

Personal Prayer

For any intimate relationship to thrive: in marriage, with friends and within families, the people involved must make that relationship a priority. Friends take time to be together. Communication is important to them. When one person is hurting or going through a difficult experience, the other is there to help and support. They share their joys, sorrows, hopes, and disappointments. Friends often join one another in hobbies or recreational activities. Together, they plan things and work on common goals. With close friends, there is a mutual desire to deepen the relationship continually.

It is no different regarding our friendship with Jesus. If we value our relationship with the Lord, we have to make Him the priority in our lives. We do this by spending time with Him in prayer.

There are a variety of ways to enter into prayer. We may simply enter God's presence and listen to Him in our hearts. We might pray the Rosary or meditate on a passage of Scripture. We could sing God's praises aloud or communicate interiorly. Our prayer life will ebb and flow; there will be times of consolation and times of dryness. But, as in any close relationship, we must remain committed to praying, regardless of how we feel or what our circumstances are.[67]

---

[66] Sheen, *Treasure in Clay*, 199.

[67] The personal-prayer suggestions offered in this paragraph do not in any way exempt us from the obligations given to us by the Church, such as attending Sunday Mass.

Develop Your Personal Prayer Life

What Flows from the Relationship

No one gets to Heaven without first becoming a saint. Many of us believe that we will finally achieve our sainthood through the cleansing of Purgatory — a tremendous spiritual blessing. But we are to strive for holiness *in this life*. And it is possible. Life, no matter how exciting, difficult, or mundane, continually offers opportunities for our spiritual growth and sanctification. But it must always be partnered with prayer, which puts us in communication with God. All we do, all our good works ought to flow out of our relationship with Jesus. If not, all the good we appear to accomplish will fall short of its spiritual benefit. Our Holy Father Pope Francis points this out:

> We can walk as much as we want, we can build many things, but if we do not profess Jesus Christ, things go wrong. We may become a charitable NGO [nongovernmental organization] but not the Church, the Bride of the Lord.[68]

Jesus and His Mission

Retreating from the world to be with His Father was important to Jesus and fundamental to His mission: "for I have come down from heaven, not to do my own will, but the will of him who sent me" (John 6:38).

> And after he had dismissed the crowds, he went up into the hills by himself to pray. (Matt. 14:23)

> And in the morning, a great while before day, he rose and went out to a lonely place, and there he prayed. (Mark 1:35)

---

[68] Pope Francis, "Missa Pro Ecclesia" with the Cardinal Electors, March 14, 2013.

We too must take time apart with God if we hope to discern and carry out His will in our lives. Sometimes we have to get creative to make it work. For busy moms, personal prayer might take place during the children's naptime or while nursing a baby. Some might pray in an adoration chapel or during a hike in the woods. Others might post a "Do not disturb" sign on the office door and turn off the phone during lunch hour in order to pray. However we fit it in, one thing is for sure: there's no substitute for quiet time with the Lord.

Spending five to ten minutes one on one with God every day, *until it becomes a habit*, is effective. Such a brief time might seem insignificant, but when we *first* firmly establish that small but doable habit, we are much more likely to be successful in our prayer life. After all, we are creatures of habit: God made us that way. Why not leverage that aspect of our human nature toward spiritual growth?

Before long, we'll find ourselves wondering how we got along without our daily prayer. Five minutes will turn into fifteen and then an hour. We'll marvel at how the time goes by so quickly. We will look forward to it and come to a point where we wouldn't miss it for anything. And when our schedules fill up and something needs to be cut, our time with the Lord will be fiercely guarded. But the small, seemingly insignificant habit usually comes first.

Distractions and Challenges

After a long day, Saint Pope John XXIII would pray, "Lord, it's your Church; I'm going to bed."[69] This very wise man turned

---

[69] Edward S. Little, *Joy in Disguise: Meeting Jesus in the Dark Times* (Harrisburg, PA: Morehouse Publishing, 2009), 130.

everything over to God in order to get his much-needed sleep. The same can be done when we turn off our electronics in order to pray. This can be a challenge in our technologically noisy culture. That innocent ping or vibration that lets us know we have a message waiting can sabotage us. The first time or two we disconnect might be uncomfortable, but that needling feeling will go away and be replaced with relief and peace. Like Pope John XXIII, we can trust God to take care of matters when we are temporarily unavailable to our coworkers, friends, and family.

Another challenge we must contend with is our busy minds. From his *Life Is Worth Living* television show, Archbishop Fulton Sheen illustrated this struggle by sharing a story about Saint Bernard.

> Saint Bernard had a friend once who told him he never had any distractions. Saint Bernard confessed to having trouble with them. The two were out horseback riding when Saint Bernard said, "I will give you this horse, if you can say the Our Father without distraction. Now, get off your horse and say the Our Father." His friend got as far as the words, "Give us this day our daily bread", when he looked up at Saint Bernard and asked, "Can I have the saddle too?"[70]

It can seem as if we are at war with our own thoughts. Not only that, but there is also a temptation to believe that our efforts are fruitless. There is a battle going on. *The Catechism of the Catholic Church* acknowledges this:

---

[70] Archbishop Fulton J. Sheen, *Life Is Worth Living* (San Francisco: Ignatius Press, 2011), 273.

The habitual difficulty in prayer is distraction.... To set about hunting down distractions would be to fall into their trap, when all that is necessary is to turn back to our heart: for a distraction reveals to us what we are attached to, and this humble awareness before the Lord should awaken our preferential love for him and lead us resolutely to offer him our heart to be purified. Therein lies the battle, the choice of which master to serve. (CCC 2729)

In the battle of prayer we must confront erroneous conceptions of prayer, various currents of thought, and our own experience of failure. We must respond with humility, trust, and perseverance to these temptations which cast doubt on the usefulness or even the possibility of prayer. (CCC 2753)

Saint Thérèse of Lisieux did not worry about her shortcomings. Her biggest challenge was staying awake during prayer. For seven years she was not able to stay awake during certain times of prayer. Thérèse did not let that discourage her. Instead, like a little child, she trusted Jesus.

I should be desolate for having slept during my hours of prayer and my thanksgiving after Holy Communion; well, I am not desolate. I remember that little children are as pleasing to their parents when they are asleep as well as when they are awake.[71]

And when the saints, especially a Doctor of the Church such as Thérèse of Lisieux, share their challenges and how

---

[71] Thérèse of Lisieux, *The Story of a Soul*, 148.

they dealt with them, it can be encouraging to us who struggle with prayer.

> But when I am alone (I'm ashamed to admit), the recitation of the Rosary costs me more than one instrument of penance.... I feel that I say it so poorly. It's in vain that I attempt to meditate on the mysteries of the Rosary—I don't succeed in engaging my mind.... For a long time I was extremely sorry for this lack of devotion that surprised me, because *I love the Blessed Virgin* so much that it ought to be easy for me to pray in her honor prayers that are pleasing to her. Now I'm less sorry, because I think that since the Queen of Heaven is *my Mother*, she must see my good will and is happy with it.[72]

What It's Really All About

Saint Faustina Kowalska tells us how important it is for everyone to pray:

> In whatever state the soul may be, it ought to pray. A soul which is pure and beautiful must pray, or else it will lose its beauty; a soul which is striving after this purity must pray, or else it will never attain it; a soul which is newly converted must pray, or else it will fall again; a sinful soul, plunged in sins, must pray so that it might rise again. There is no soul which is not bound to pray, for every single grace comes to the soul through prayer. (*Diary*, no. 146)

We are totally dependent on God's grace. We could not hope to pray or make any progress in the spiritual life without

[72] Ibid., 219.

God's help. However, our participation is required. Even so, no matter what we do, it will never be enough—God does it all. It is, therefore, appropriate that we approach prayer with humility.

> Humility is the foundation of prayer.... The baptized person should train himself to live in humility. (CCC 2540)

☞

Reflection

Prayer is not about getting a specific devotion accomplished each day or a particular style of communing with God. It is not about emulating a certain saint or being like someone else. Prayer has everything to do with our relationship with the Lord. Our personal prayer time is unique for each of us, and it will change and develop as we do.

Sometimes we just do not know how to begin. Or we may need to jumpstart our existing prayer life. In the *Catechism* we find an efficacious yet simple method of prayer that we can always employ.

> But the one name that contains everything is the one that the Son of God received in his incarnation: JESUS. The divine name may not be spoken by human lips, but by assuming our humanity. The Word of God hands it over to us and we can invoke it: "Jesus," "YHWH saves." The name "Jesus" contains all: God and man and the whole economy of creation and salvation. To pray, "Jesus" is to invoke him and to call him within us. His name is the only one that contains the presence it signifies. Jesus is the Risen One, and whoever invokes the name of Jesus is

welcoming the Son of God who loved him and who gave himself up for him....

The invocation of the holy name of Jesus is the simplest way of praying always. When the holy name is repeated often by a humbly attentive heart, the prayer is not lost by heaping up empty phrases, but holds fast to the word and "brings forth fruit with patience." This prayer is possible "at all times" because it is not one occupation among others but the only occupation: that of loving God, which animates and transfigures every action in Christ Jesus (CCC 2666, 2668).

6

Embrace Your Mission — at Any Age

*At every stage of life the Lord can ask each of us to
contribute what talents we have. The Service of
the Gospel has nothing to do with age!*

—Saint John Paul II, *Letter to the Elderly*

Wealthy and Neglected: Blessed Pier Giorgio Frassati

Pier Giorgio Frassati died on July 4, 1925. He had contracted
polio, and in a matter of days the vibrant twenty-four-year-old
was gone. His parents were in for quite a revelation regarding
their son. They did not really get to know Pier Giorgio until
after he died. And they were not the only ones. Any citizen of
Turin would have recognized the famous Frassati name, but to
the numerous poor of the city, the young man who was taken
from them so suddenly was simply their beloved Fra Girolamo.
Although the poor of Turin had not known his legal identity,
they *knew* him. He was Christ among them.

Rich and famous: this describes the Frassati family. At the
turn of the twentieth century, Pier Giorgio's father, Alfredo
Frassati, owned *La Stampa*, the daily newspaper of Turin, Italy.
Alfredo was also a well-known statesman, serving his country as
an ambassador to Germany and a senator.

Pier Giorgio's father was an agnostic. His mother, Adelaide, was a Catholic but practiced the Faith minimally. There were no prayers said at meals or at bedtime, and although Adelaide attended Sunday Mass, she never received Communion and was critical of the Church.[73]

The two parents were absorbed in their own interests. They gave scant attention to their two children, Pier Giorgio and Luciana. As young children, Pier Giorgio and Luciana were tutored at home but were not allowed to play with others their age, nor were they permitted to talk to adults. Despite the family's wealth, the children were often neglected, sometimes going hungry. The Frassati home was not a happy one. It could have been a very lonely childhood if not for the close relationship between this brother and sister.

Young Pier Giorgio possessed a natural empathy for others. He would give food or clothes to beggars who came to the door. Once he hurriedly took off his shoes, tossed them to a woman holding her unshod boy, and quickly shut the door before anyone in the house could notice.[74]

Jesus in the Eucharist Makes All the Difference
The turning point for Pier Giorgio came when he was twelve years of age. Because he had failed Latin, he was sent to a school run by Jesuit priests. The Jesuits obviously had a big influence on his spiritual formation. After attending their school for two years, he begged his mother to allow him (now fourteen) to

---

[73] Father Tim Deeter, *Blessed Pier Giorgio Frassati—Man of the Beatitudes* (Sycamore, IL: Lighthouse Catholic Media, 2011), audio CD.
[74] Ibid.

attend daily Mass. After he persisted in this request for several days, his mother reluctantly acquiesced.[75]

Pier Giorgio would walk, or run, to Mass every day. Of course, this required leaving very early in the morning and often in the dark, but always alone. From this point on, the spiritual growth for this young teen escalated and grew exponentially. Fueled by the Lord in the Eucharist, Pier Giorgio blossomed in sanctity as if it were the most natural thing for him to do.

When he was old enough, he would reconnect with the Jesuits, attending their yearly retreats and bringing friends with him. His faith was not a personal affair but something he shared with everyone in a disarming way. For instance, if he and his pals were participating in a competitive game involving betting, he would wager money if his friends would wager time — an hour at the adoration chapel. At night, on the streets of Turin, it was not unusual to see a group of teenage boys, Pier Giorgio among them, playfully jostling with one another as they made their way to the church. The friends would sometimes fall asleep during the hour's watch with our Lord. But Pier Giorgio would go to the front and kneel closest to the Blessed Sacrament, where he would become completely absorbed in prayer. When the hour was up, they all left together, resuming their lighthearted play as they traversed the streets of Turin. Pier Giorgio's friends often remarked that their own parents could not get them to church, but Pier Giorgio could.[76]

During Mass and adoration, Pier Giorgio brought his concerns to Jesus. And from the Lord he received direction and

[75] Elaine Woodfield, *An Eye on Eternity, The Life and Death of Blessed Pier Giorgio Frassati* (New York: NOOK Study, 2013), electronic edition, 24.

[76] Deeter, *Blessed Pier Giorgio Frassati.*

grace to carry out his mission. In letters to friends, he shared this great treasure:

> I urge you with all the strength of my soul to approach the Eucharist Table as often as possible. Feed on this Bread of the Angels from which you will draw the strength to fight inner struggles.[77]
>
> When you are totally consumed by the Eucharistic fire, then you will be able more consciously to thank God, who has called you to become part of His family. Then you will enjoy the peace that those who are happy in this world have never experienced.[78]

In many ways, Pier Giorgio was a typical young man. Socializing with his friends was important to him. He struggled with schoolwork and enjoyed athletics, particularly skiing and mountain climbing. He was a fun person whose exuberant personality drew others to him. For a while he had a girlfriend and considered marriage.[79]

Pier Giorgio was active in many Catholic organizations, among them the Saint Vincent de Paul Society and the Catholic Student Federation. He was a natural leader and participated in nonviolent student protests against fascism. On one occasion, this activity landed him in jail. While processing the arrests, the police discovered that Pier Giorgio was the son of the famous Alfredo Frassati. They wanted to release him, but he refused the special treatment and was interned with the other students,

---

[77] Luciana Frassati, *A Man of the Beatitudes: Pier Giorgio Frassati* (San Francisco: Ignatius Press, 2000), 122.

[78] Ibid., 132.

[79] Deeter, *Blessed Pier Giorgio Frassati*.

many of whom had been badly beaten. Pier Giorgio had been roughed up a bit, too, but he stayed with his friends, offering encouragement and comfort until their releases were arranged.

Daily Mass, the Rosary, Eucharistic adoration, and personal prayer kept Pier Giorgio connected to the Lord. Everything in the life of this young faithful disciple flowed from that divine and very personal relationship.

He was especially drawn to those people who were alone in facing their hardships. For example, when a pregnant woman whose husband was in prison needed a friend, Pier Giorgio became that friend. He accompanied her to the maternity hospital where she gave birth, and he made it possible for her to stay there as long as necessary. He was delighted when asked to be the newborn's godfather and happily provided the infant's white baptismal gown. When the woman's husband was released, Pier Giorgio met him at the prison gate. He escorted the man to a factory where Pier Giorgio had secured a job for him.[80]

When accompanying Pier Giorgio on a hospital visit, a friend observed:

> He would wander through the corridors with a secure and steady spirit of charity, consoling the wretched and stopping to talk to them as though they were really his brothers. He would bring them money, candy, and clothes, and would never forget to kiss them warmly as though they were the closest of friends, not even stopping to think of the possible risk of infection or having any hint of human repulsion.[81]

---

[80] Woodfield, *An Eye on Eternity*, 46.
[81] Ibid.

Attracted to the Dominican Order's contemplation-in-action approach to life, Pier Giorgio became a Third Order Dominican, taking the name Fra (Brother) Girolamo.[82] Concealing the prestigious Frassati name, the poor of Turin knew him simply as Fra Girolamo.

After Pier Giorgio's death, the family expected Turin's elite as well as Pier Giorgio's friends to attend his funeral. Imagine their surprise when, in addition to the expected guests, the streets were lined with thousands of mourners. The poor of Turin, who must have also been stunned to find that their beloved Fra Girolamo was from the famous Frassati family, came out in droves to pay their respects.

Given Pier Giorgio's upbringing and environment, it is quite remarkable to realize the degree of holiness he achieved in his short twenty-four years on this earth. He was given many tasks by the Lord and was perpetually *on a mission*, often juggling several simultaneously. Pier Giorgio Frassati, lovingly known as Fra Girolamo, behaved as if he did not have much time on this earth, and indeed, he did not.

Mission Accomplished

There are few who would dispute that throughout his life, Pope John Paul II was given several missions from God. Not all at once, of course, but he received a seemingly endless stream of varied and weighty tasks to be accomplished in God's plan. There was, however, one mission that he considered his special task.[83]

---

[82] Girolamo Savonarola was a controversial fifteenth-century Dominican friar. Pier Giorgio explained, "I am a fervent admirer of this friar, who died as a saint at the stake."

[83] John Paul II, at the Shrine of Merciful Love in Collevalenza, Italy, November 22, 1981.

Right from the beginning of my ministry in St. Peter's See in Rome, I consider this message [of Divine Mercy] my special task. Providence has assigned it to me in the present situation of man, the Church and the world. It could be said that precisely this situation assigned that message to me as my task before God.[84]

The message of Divine Mercy has always been near and dear to me. [I took it] with me to the See of Peter and ... in a sense [it] forms the image of this pontificate.[85]

At the dawn of the third millennium, humanity was, and still is, in great need of hope, healing, fortification, and, above all these graces, mercy. The twentieth-century Church had come through several horrific persecutions around the world. There were more Catholics martyred in that bloody century than all other previous centuries combined.[86]

The Lord, of course, always provides for the wounds caused by sinful humanity: "where sin increased, grace abounded all the more" (Rom. 5:20). This He did through His Divine Mercy message of mercy, hope, and healing given to the Polish nun Sister Faustina Kowalska. The message of Divine Mercy, along with the devotions taught to Sister Faustina by our Lord Jesus, passed through a time of investigation and testing. Although the devotion was spreading, there was more to be done if this profound message, which was given for this particular time in history, was to have an impact on the world. Therefore, on the

---

[84] Ibid.

[85] John Paul II, "Apostolic Journey, Shrine of Divine Mercy," June 7, 1997.

[86] "The 20th Century Saw 65 Percent of Christian Martyrs," EWTN News, May 10, 2002.

Second Sunday of Easter in 2000, Pope John Paul II completed the mission. The Holy Father canonized Saint Faustina Kowalska and fulfilled Jesus' request by inaugurating the first Divine Mercy Sunday.[87]

God is merciful, and we must trust Him: that is essentially the Divine Mercy message given to Sister Faustina by Jesus. It sounds simple, almost trite, but when we realize the *extent* of His mercy, it is truly amazing. However, there is also a sense of urgency to the message. "You will prepare the world for My final coming" (*Diary*, no. 429) are the words of Jesus to the simple Polish nun. Before He comes as the just Judge, Jesus wants no one to escape His merciful love. He instructed Faustina:

> Speak to the world about My mercy.... It is a sign for the end times. After it will come the Day of Justice. While there is still time, let them have recourse to the fountain of My mercy. (*Diary*, no. 848)

In the message, we are taught how to appropriate God's grace and mercy for others and ourselves. It's all about saving souls! This message of Divine Mercy is so remarkable that it mystifies the angels.

> There are moments and there are mysteries of the divine mercy over which the heavens are astounded. Let our judgment of souls cease, for God's mercy upon them is extraordinary. (*Diary*, no. 1684)

Most telling, however, is a comment John Paul II made at a banquet held after the ceremonies on that first Divine Mercy

---

[87] You can find extensive resources and information about the Divine Mercy message at www.TheDivineMercy.org.

Sunday. He said, "This is the happiest day of my life!" Certainly in the life of Saint John Paul II, there were days of tremendous accomplishments and much celebration. His election as pope, the fall of Communism in Poland, or the surprise reunion with a close friend whom he had believed dead could all be contenders for what made the happiest day of his life. The list of possibilities could be quite long. But establishing the feast of Divine Mercy, canonizing Saint Faustina, and delivering the Divine Mercy message to the entire world—that was his *happiest day*. Why? It's simple really, and it's the same for everyone. We are happiest and most fulfilled when we are truly doing God's will. Pope John Paul II had accomplished his mission, and he rejoiced in it.

Called into the Father's Vineyard at Any Hour

God calls us to participate in His divine work. He invites us to respond at *any hour of our lives* as demonstrated by Jesus in His parable of the laborers in the vineyard.

> For the kingdom of heaven is like a landowner who went out early in the morning to hire laborers for his vineyard. After agreeing with the laborers for the usual daily wage, he sent them into his vineyard. When he went out about nine o'clock, he saw others standing idle in the marketplace; and he said to them, "You also go into the vineyard, and I will pay you whatever is right." So they went. When he went out again about noon and about three o'clock, he did the same. And about five o'clock he went out and found others standing around; and he said to them, "Why are you standing here idle all day?" They said to him, "Because no one has hired us." He said to them, "You also go into the vineyard."

When evening came, the owner of the vineyard said to his manager, "Call the laborers and give them their pay, beginning with the last and then going to the first." When those hired about five o'clock came, each of them received the usual daily wage. Now when the first came, they thought they would receive more; but each of them also received the usual daily wage. And when they received it, they grumbled against the landowner, saying, "These last worked only one hour, and you have made them equal to us who have borne the burden of the day and the scorching heat." But he replied to one of them, "Friend, I am doing you no wrong; did you not agree with me for the usual daily wage? Take what belongs to you and go; I choose to give to this last the same as I give to you. Am I not allowed to do what I choose with what belongs to me? Or are you envious because I am generous?"

So the last will be first, and the first will be last. (Matt 20:1–16)

This parable is the basis for Pope John Paul II's apostolic exhortation *Chrisifdeles Laici* (*The Vocation and Mission of the Lay Faithful in the Church and the World*). Throughout the exhortation, the pope tells all people, especially the laity:

Go into the Father's vineyard. Each person should take into account what he does and consider if he is laboring in the vineyard of the Lord.[88]

It's not too late to embrace the mission God has given and go into the vineyard of the Lord. We cannot make up for lost

---

[88] John Paul II, *Christifideles Laici*, no. 2.

time; it is impossible to go back and relive any moment. That is why this message of hope, especially when we focus on those last-hour laborers, is so fabulous. God is incredibly charitable.

There are times when finding God's will for our lives can be puzzling. After all, how does anyone *hear the voice of God?* Pope John Paul II gives us some very practical advice:

> To be able to discover the actual will of the Lord in our lives always involves the following:
>
> • a receptive listening to the word of God and the Church
>
> • fervent and constant prayer
>
> • recourse to a wise and loving spiritual guide
>
> • a faithful discernment of the gifts and talents given by God, as well as the diverse social and historic situations in which one lives[89]

Discovering God's will is only the first step. We must be willing to follow through on what He asks of us.

> It is not a question of simply *knowing* what God wants from each of us in the various situations of life. The individual must *do* what God wants, as we are reminded in the words that Mary, the Mother of Jesus, addressed to the servants at Cana: "Do whatever he tells you" (Jn 2:5).[90]

The Holy Father tells us that during our formation as Christians we can expect:

> an ever-clearer discovery of one's vocation and the ever-greater willingness to live it so as to fulfill one's mission.

---

[89] Ibid., no. 58.
[90] Ibid.

He clarifies by telling us: In life ... there are particularly significant and decisive moments for discerning God's call and embracing the mission entrusted by Him.... No one must forget that the Lord, as the master of the laborers in the vineyard, calls at every hour of life so as to make his holy will more precisely and explicitly known.[91]

Could *now* be one of those "particularly significant and decisive moments"? God put us on earth at this time in history and in our own circumstances for His particular reasons.

The Holy Father continues by reinforcing the necessity of prayer and listening,

Therefore, the fundamental and continuous attitude of the disciple should be one of vigilance and a conscious attentiveness to the voice of God.[92]

But do we think that we are too old, too young, too ... ? From the beginning, people have been making excuses and trying to prove that they aren't up to the task given them by God. We have only to look at some of the major Old Testament characters to see that human nature hasn't changed.

From our vantage point, it seems almost impossible that anyone who had seen signs and wonders performed by God, or had spoken with the Lord face-to-face, as Moses did (Exod. 33:11), would doubt the Lord's wisdom. But we often see Old Testament characters explaining to God why they cannot do the job He has asked of them.

Moses was a great objector. "Who am I?... I am slow of speech and of tongue" (Exod. 3:11; 4:10).

---

[91] John Paul II, *Christifideles Laici*, no. 58.
[92] Ibid.

Jeremiah's protest is similar, "I do not know how to speak, for I am only a youth" (Jer. 1:6).

We, on the other hand, have the fulfillment of the New Testament in Jesus Christ. We have the Church guided by the Holy Spirit. And we have the most miraculous signs and wonders of all — the sacraments. The figures of the Old Testament could legitimately point to us and say, "If we had known what you know, we would never have doubted the Lord's designs!"

We have heard the saying, "The Lord does not call the qualified; He qualifies the called." Looking at it this way, we see that many of the main characters in salvation history appeared *uniquely unqualified.* Abraham was an old man; King David was an adulterer; Saint Peter denied Jesus; and Saint Paul (then known as Saul) was a murderer of Christians.

We can come up with all kinds of excuses. But, if God calls us, He will provide for our shortcomings.

> However, to act in fidelity to God's will requires a capability for acting and the developing of that capability. We can rest assured that this is possible through the free and responsible collaboration of each of us with the grace of the Lord which is never lacking.[93]

John Paul II had this to say regarding the objections based on age:

> At every stage of life the Lord can ask each of us to contribute what talents we have. The Service of the Gospel has nothing to do with age![94]

---

[93] Ibid.
[94] John Paul II, *Letter to the Elderly,* no. 7.

What if our mission, our calling, by all appearances, is to *do nothing*? Well, it might look as if we are doing nothing because of the limitations placed on us through illness or old age. But the opposite can be true when we join our situation to Jesus' redemptive work on the Cross. Suffering (no matter what type or how small) is a mission of the highest order. Saint Paul confirms this:

> [I]n my flesh I complete what is lacking in Christ's afflictions for the sake of his body, that is, the church. (Col. 1:24)

Our Lady told the children at Fatima, "Many souls go to hell because they have no one to pray and make sacrifices for them." Some of the most meaningful work—through which souls can be won or lost for all eternity—is done in a sickbed. Those who do this work by offering their sufferings for others are *chosen souls*. Jesus explained this to Sister Faustina Kowalska:

> Chosen souls are, in My hand, lights which I cast into the darkness of the world and with which I illuminate it. As stars illumine the night, so chosen souls illuminate the earth. And the more perfect a soul is, the stronger and more far-reaching is the light shed by it. It can be hidden and unknown, even to those closest to it, and yet its holiness is reflected in souls even to the most distant extremities of the world. (*Diary*, no. 1601)

To those who feel they have lost their usefulness and especially to the elderly, John Paul had this to say:

> The Church still needs you.... She appreciates the services which you may wish to provide in many areas of

the apostolate; she counts on the support of your longer periods of prayer; she counts on your advice born of experience, and she is enriched by your daily witness to the Gospel.[95]

In Pope John Paul's *Letter to the Elderly*, he emphasizes that all the phases of life have their particular character and that every phase is a meaningful preparation for eternity. In the letter, he recounts the different periods of his life, drawing lessons from his own personal history. Just as John Paul II reached out to the many different groups (the youth, families, women, et cetera), he wrote this particular letter to the elderly with a deep desire to connect with them.

> As an older person myself, I have felt the desire to engage in a conversation with you.[96] I feel a spontaneous desire to share fully with you my own feelings at this point of my life, after more than twenty years of ministry on the throne of Peter and as we await the arrival, now imminent, of the Third Millennium. Despite the limitations brought on by age, I continue to enjoy life. For this I thank the Lord.[97]

Let's hope and pray that whether we are young or old, rich or poor, gifted or challenged, healthy or infirm, we will be able to say truthfully with Pope Saint John Paul II: "It is wonderful to be able to give oneself to the very end for the sake of the kingdom of God!"[98]

---

[95] John Paul II, *Letter to the Elderly*, no. 13.
[96] Ibid., no. 17.
[97] Ibid.
[98] Ibid.

⌢

Reflection

During his papacy, John Paul II taught this truth to many different groups of people: *we each have an irreplaceable part in God's plan*. Whatever our particular mission is, it contributes in some way to saving souls — our own and others. Remember what Saint Paul tells about our different functions in the Body of Christ.

> Now there are varieties of gifts, but the same Spirit; and there are varieties of service, but the same Lord; and there are varieties of working, but it is the same God who inspires them all in every one....
>
> Now you are the body of Christ and individually members of it. And God has appointed in the church first apostles, second prophets, third teachers, then workers of miracles, then healers, helpers, administrators, speakers in various kinds of tongues. Are all apostles? Are all prophets? Are all teachers? Do all work miracles? Do all possess gifts of healing? Do all speak with tongues? Do all interpret? (1 Cor. 12: 4–6, 27–30)

7

Rely on God to Get It Right
When You Get It Wrong

Things were in God's plan which I had not planned at all. I am coming to the living faith and conviction that—from God's point of view—there is no chance and that the whole of my life, down to every detail, has been mapped out in God's divine providence and makes complete and perfect sense in God's all-seeing eyes.

—Saint Teresa Benedicta of the Cross (Edith Stein)

One Hundred Eighty Degrees in the Wrong Direction: Blessed Bartolo Longo

One evening he was consecrated "priest of spiritualism" in a strange, macabre ceremony, in the midst of black drapes, skulls of the dead and crossed shin bones. He advanced bare-footed, wearing a black cloak.... He recited certain formulas.... He was anointed with oil.... He gave a magnificent proof of falling into a trance, responding to questions and invoking first Pythagoras, then Confucius, and then Caiaphas.... Spiritualism had a new "priest," with a body reduced to skin and bones, two possessed eyes, [and] frazzled nerves.[99]

While studying law at the University of Naples, Bartolo Longo lost his faith in the one, holy, catholic, and apostolic Church. The eloquent professors under whom Bartolo studied were imbued with a hatred for the Church and especially the authority of the pope. These articulate men were persuasive, passionate, and highly motivated in leading students away from all things Catholic. Later in life, Bartolo wrote about it:

> Overwhelmed as I was in the ebullience of my youth, in the errors against the faith and against the True Church as sown in the celebrated University of Naples ... ensnared on the enticing hook of freedom of conscience and thought ... feeling secure in the reverberations of certain professors' names echoing as far as the universities of Paris and of Berlin ... all in agreement in denying the person of God, the Catholic Church, the religious orders, the Pope, the sacraments and the rest of truth which is part of faith, I too grew to hate monks, priests, and the pope.[100]

During Bartolo's university years in the early 1860s, Europe was experiencing the unholy advance of spiritualism and occultism. It was not enough for the young law student simply to reject the Church. Bartolo hungered for truth. Since he was convinced that truth could not be found in the Catholic Church, he looked for it in the opposite direction.

---

[99] Ann M. Brown, *Apostle of the Rosary: Blessed Bartolo Longo* (New Hope, KY: New Hope Publications, 2004), 11.
[100] Ibid., 8.

Rely on God to Get It Right

In 1864, Bartolo attended his first séance. During the unholy exchange, the inquisitive university student asked the entranced medium some questions:

Is Jesus Christ God?

[The answer:] Yes.

Does hell exist?

No.

Are the precepts of the Decalogue true?

All of them, except the sixth.[101]

Unlike so many who are attracted to the occult because of the phenomena associated with it, such as strange voices, moving objects, and weird displays of power, Bartolo was searching for knowledge that continued beyond this life. He wanted to know spiritualism's doctrine of salvation. The medium answered with just enough truth seriously to excite the naive young man. When looking back on that initial séance, Bartolo wrote, "I believed I had finally found the path that would lead me to the truth."

Pope Paul VI explains Satan's strategies. In Bartolo's case, the evil tactics had been very effective in turning the young man away from the truth he was seeking:

> He [Satan] undermines man's moral equilibrium with his sophistry. He is the malign, clever seducer who knows how to make his way into us through the senses, the imagination and the libido, through utopian logic, or through disordered social contacts in the give and take of our activities, so that he can bring about in us deviations

---

[101] Brown, *Apostle of the Rosary*, 10. The Sixth Commandment in the Catholic version is "You shall not commit adultery."

that are all the more harmful because they seem to conform to our physical or mental makeup, or to our profound, instinctive aspirations.[102]

Being an enthusiastic, all-or-nothing kind of person, Bartolo threw himself into spiritualism. He was not satisfied to seek the spirits through mediums: he wanted direct access. He therefore consecrated himself to Satan and became a "minister of the spirit."[103]

Immediately following his pact with the devil, Bartolo's life disintegrated in multiple ways. He was sad but not in a usual way one might be sad about something. It was an ever-present oppressive sadness.

And he was confused. His spirit companion whom he called his "angel" gave inconsistent answers to the questions that were so important to him. These, too, contradicted the replies received from other "ministers of the spirit." Their "angels" did not agree with his or each other.

Bartolo's physical health was suffering: his appearance was wild and haunting, unrecognizable by those who had known him before. His mental state was taxed almost beyond his strength, with his grip on sanity slipping.

Delivered from Darkness
Bartolo's failing health and apparent anxiety did not escape the notice of one of his professors, Vincenzo Pepe, one of the few

---

[102] John LaBriola, *Onward Catholic Soldier: Spiritual Warfare according to Scripture, the Church, and the Saints* (Orange, CA: Luke 1:38 Publishing, 2008), 163.

[103] Ibid.

remaining loyal Catholics at the University of Naples. Professor Pepe warned Bartolo that his association with spiritualism and the occult would land him in the "madhouse."[104]

The wise Catholic faculty member then implemented a most strategic move: he solicited prayers from many other Catholics for Bartolo. Without Bartolo's knowledge or consent, a spiritual war was being waged on his behalf. The prize was nothing less than the most valuable thing that any human being possesses—his eternal soul.

The decisive moment came when Bartolo mentioned to Professor Pepe that he had contacted the spirit of his deceased father. As a result, Bartolo had decided to have a Mass offered for his father's soul. This was a prime example of the inconsistencies and confusion that Bartolo was experiencing. Only in this case, the young man was clueless and did not see the apparent contradiction.

On hearing this, Professor Pepe, inspired with zeal for God and a deep concern for the soul of his young friend, made a bold move. He demanded, "Not only will you have a Mass said, but you will also make your confession to one of those learned and holy monks. Tomorrow—understand?"[105]

Remarkably, Bartolo agreed.

After a month of daily meetings with the Dominican priest Father Radente, Bartolo was reconciled to the Church. A time of purification and spiritual growth followed. Bartolo regularly practiced the Corporal Works of Mercy, developed a consistent prayer life that included a Rosary group, and studied theology. After a period of formation, he was received as a member of

[104] Ibid., 12.
[105] Ibid.

the Dominican Third Order on the feast of the Holy Rosary, October 7, 1871.

A Great Mission, Then Another and Another . . .

During a trip to Pompeii, Bartolo was taken aback when he learned how ignorant the peasants were about the Catholic Faith. Only 5 percent of the two thousand inhabitants attended Mass at the poorly kept, vermin-infested church.[106] Although he had come to the Valley of Pompeii to take care of a business transaction for a friend, Bartolo was deeply concerned about the skewed ideas and mixture of Christian doctrine with superstition. What he found even more troubling was the infusion of occult practices in the lives of the people. The local Catholics were as confused as he had once been; they readily sought the services of witches and mediums. He decided to go for a walk to consider the situation.

While on that walk, the demonic influences of his past assailed him with a vengeance. He was overcome with anguish and suicidal thoughts. He began to tell himself that because of his past, particularly his consecration to Satan, he was worthless and good for nothing. His soul was in torment — the struggle intense. It was then that the advice of Father Radente came to mind:

> If you are looking for salvation, propagate the Rosary. It is Mary's promise: whoever propagates the Rosary will be saved.

Bartolo describes what happened next:

> I then prostrated myself and my eyes filled with tears. With the boldness of desperation I lifted my face and hands to the Heavenly Virgin and cried, "If it be true

---

[106] O'Neel, *39 New Saints You Should Know*, 96–97.

that you promised St. Dominic that whoever spreads the
Rosary will be saved, I will be saved, because I shall not
depart from this land of Pompeii without having spread
your Rosary."[107]

Blessed Bartolo Longo was true to his word. In his propagation of the Rosary and his great love for the Virgin Mary, he
accomplished several missions in the "land of Pompeii." The
most notable and well known is the construction of the Pontifi-
cal Shrine of the Blessed Virgin of the Rosary of Pompeii. Later
he wrote of his motivations:

> We [he and those who shared his vision for the peasants
> of Pompeii] wanted only to provide for the religious life
> of poor peasants. We succeeded in producing a truly uni-
> versal movement of faith, a Catholic movement, Catholic
> [that is, universal] just as the Church is.[108]

When there is a resurgence of faith, there is a building up
of society. Bartolo's ministry to catechize the people and spread
devotion to the Rosary resulted in the establishment of schools
for poor children, orphanages, and trade schools.

In order to keep pilgrims and devotees informed of the many
miracles and stories associated with the shrine (in 1885 alone,
there were 940 cures recorded), Bartolo started a magazine, *The
Rosary and the New Pompeii*. This publication became the largest
journal in the country. Bartolo wrote:

> Ah, my God, you did not look at my past, you did not
> stop before my weakness; in one hand you placed a rosary,

---

[107] Brown, *Apostle of the Rosary*, 21.
[108] O'Neel, *39 New Saints You Should Know*, 97.

in the other a pen, and you said to me: Write, they will listen to you, for it is I who will place in your heart the word of life.[109]

There were nevertheless, the trials to endure. Regardless of his accomplishments and the outward proof of his fidelity, Bartolo's motives and reputation were continually questioned. His close association with Countess de Fusco (who was involved in the various ministries and fundraising associated with the shrine) was the cause of rumors. To avoid scandal and at the urging of Pope Leo XIII, they married (this was later in life), but remained celibate. For a time, the pope, who had been misinformed, questioned Bartolo's honesty when handling donations to the shrine. This was perhaps the most sorrowful cross for Bartolo. His response was always silence as he continued to embrace yet another mission given to him from above.

The rumors were plentiful when he decided to build a home for the sons of prisoners, educate them, and apprentice them in the shrine's printing shop. These unfortunate boys were seen as hopeless causes destined to become criminals themselves. One news source wrote: "The moralist cannot approve, the sociologist must protest.... This new shelter in the Valley of Pompeii threatens to become a nest of delinquents."

Of course they were wrong. After fifteen years, Bartolo was able to report:

Today one hundred prisoners' sons are living in this home. One hundred and three have already been sent away as well-educated boys or have been taken in by honest and secure families. We have received good news concerning

---

[109] Brown, *Apostle of the Rosary*, 97.

all of them. They are scattered about in workshops, in the clergy, in the army, in the royal navy, in military bands; and many of them have even crossed to the distant shores of America.[110]

Bartolo's confidence was not misplaced. The first prisoner's son to arrive in his orphanage became a priest and celebrated his first Mass at the altar of Our Lady of Pompeii.

When asked how he managed to do so well with these high-risk boys, Blessed Bartolo Longo replied, "I gave them, and taught them to love, Jesus Christ."[111]

No matter how misguided our search for the truth or how ugly our past, when we turn to God and offer him our broken lives, He works miracles. We can get it wrong, *seriously wrong*, but if we turn to the Lord (often repeatedly), He will show us what His will is for our lives. And He will give us the grace to carry out any mission that He asks of us. Blessed Bartolo Longo is proof par excellence!

God Gets Us There

"What was I thinking?" Have you ever asked yourself this question after doing something really stupid? Most of us have — on multiple occasions. Sometimes, though, even with the best intentions, a thorough investigation of the decision at hand, seeking wise counsel, and boatloads of prayer, we can still miss the mark.

When Saint Francis of Assisi heard the Lord tell him, "Rebuild my Church," Francis immediately went to work rebuilding the physical church at San Damiano, an ancient chapel on

---

[110] Ibid., 36–38.
[111] Ibid., 37.

the verge of collapse. It seemed obvious to the obedient young Francis that the church at San Damiano was the object of his instructions from the Lord. Of course, there were larger implications to the message, and in time, Francis figured it out. But his enthusiastic response demonstrates that even if a person hears the voice of God, he might misunderstand and initially get it wrong.

We might not find this story encouraging. After all, if a holy man such as Saint Francis could get the wrong idea, what hope is there for us? The answer is not so much in knowing, but in trusting. The knowing comes in time — God's time. The trusting is an act of our will that most of us need to reassert again and again. As long as we are seeking His will and relying on His guidance, our Lord will take care of the rest; He'll get us where we need to be.

We might say, "That's easier said than done." True ... and not true. It all depends on our purity of intention. A question to ask is: "Whose will are we really seeking? Ours or God's?" We are masterfully skilled at camouflaging our own self-serving interests; we can even fool ourselves. Here's one example of such a deception regarding prayer — and it comes from Jesus:

> And when you pray, you must not be like the hypocrites;
> for they love to stand and pray in the synagogues and at
> the street corners, that they may be seen by men. Truly, I
> say to you, they have their reward. (Matt. 6:5)

Those men praying in the synagogues and on the street corners believed their prayers were pleasing to God. They were duped — not by others or even by the devil, but by themselves! Their performances were not about prayer or a relationship with God. Rather, their aim was religious notoriety: those men wanted to be recognized for their holiness. But in reality, they personi-fied the direct opposite of what they believed themselves to be.

Quite often it's not that cut-and-dried. Those hypocrites could have sincerely wanted both to enter into prayer *and* to glean recognition, but the duplicity of their intention was their undoing. So let's not be too judgmental; many of us can easily find ourselves on the disingenuous side, with a foot in each camp.

For instance, have we ever participated in charity work, sin-cerely happy to be helping (good intention), but secretly hoping that others, or a particular person, would notice us as well (du-plicity of intention)? Are we always interested in a relationship because of the friendship, or is there also some benefit in it for us: perhaps recognition or a financial advantage? Scrutinizing our motives can be applied to all the areas of our lives in an effort to ensure our pure intentions. But when it comes to our relationship with the Lord, this self-examination is especially important. Just like the hypocrites in Matthew's Gospel, we can fool others and even ourselves, but we can't fool Jesus.

So what does He tell us to do? "But when you pray, go into your room and shut the door and pray to your Father who is in secret; and your Father who sees in secret will reward you" (Matt. 6:6).

So yes, having purity of intention can be (and usually is) an ongoing challenge. We must continually battle our built-in propensity to sin, our concupiscence. The solution is a simple formula: $W + w = S$.

Big Goals: Saint Maximilian Kolbe

Saint Maximilian Kolbe authored and taught $W + w = S$. The capital W stands for God's will, the small w stands for our will, and the capital S stands for sanctity. Attaining sainthood was

Maximilian's goal from early on. Shortly before his ordination to the priesthood, Maximilian formulated his goals and put them in writing. Number one on his list was, "I wish to be a saint and a *great* saint."[112]

Indeed, Saint Maximilian Kolbe achieved his number-one goal. He is most commonly known for his heroic sacrifice at Auschwitz, where he took the place of another prisoner condemned to death by starvation. His courageous witness embodied Jesus' two greatest commandments:

> "You shall love the Lord your God with all your heart, and with all your soul, and with all your mind." This is the great and first commandment. And a second is like it, "You shall love your neighbor as yourself." (Matt. 22:37–39)

Based on his simple formula, we might be tempted to think that Maximilian, although certainly holy, might not necessarily be too sophisticated or educated. Nothing could be further from the truth. Maximilian had an exceptional mind, a love for learning, and a strong bent toward mathematics and physics, earning two PhDs before his twenty-fifth birthday. But like Einstein with his $E=mc^2$,[113] genius has a way of distilling hard-to-grasp realities into understandable and uncomplicated terms. Kolbe's formula for sainthood may be simple, but it is profound.

Possessing a childlike faith and believing nothing was impossible with Mary Immaculate, Father Maximilian Kolbe produced

---

[112] Patricia Treece, *A Man for Others: Maximilian Kolbe Saint of Auschwitz, in the Words of Those Who Knew Him* (Huntington, IN: Our Sunday Visitor, 1982), 67.

[113] Energy equals mass times the speed of light squared.

a printing apostolate that was nothing short of amazing for his day and time. At its height, the friary, Niepokalanów, had become an almost self-sufficient little town with 694 inhabitants, numerous buildings, a variety of tradesmen, a fire department, a lumberyard, a fleet of trucks for distribution, a fleet of bicycles, and an infirmary. There were several printing presses, which produced a daily paper and eleven magazines, and a radio station. No other media outlet impacted the Polish people more than Father Maximilian Kolbe and his friars.

Maximilian's talents and heart were in total service to the Immaculata, the "Immaculate One," his favorite name for Mary. He and his friars wanted nothing less than to *save the entire world* for Jesus through Mary Immaculate and, to that end, there was continual planning. At the time of the German invasion, there were plans to build a paper mill and an airfield so his friars (they were in flight training), could distribute the magazines and newspapers farther and more efficiently. All this, as well as the establishment of a mission and printing apostolate in Nagasaki, Japan, was done before the Nazi invasion of Poland, which led to his martyrdom.

The Militia Immaculata

From an early age Raymond Kolbe (his given name; he would receive the name Maximilian in the seminary) loved the Blessed Mother. She had appeared to him during his childhood, offering him two crowns, one of purity and one of martyrdom. When asked which crown he wanted, young Raymond chose both.

When it comes to spiritual gifts, Saint Paul tells us to go for it! This is the one area where we are encouraged to want more. "But earnestly desire the higher gifts," "the spiritual gifts" (1 Cor. 12:31; 14:1). We see this attitude manifested when young Raymond takes both crowns offered and when seminarian

Maximilian sets his goals down on paper: "I wish to be a saint, and a *great* saint."[114]

During his formative years in the seminary, Maximilian often spoke of consecrating his entire life to a great idea. In 1915, when he was just twenty-three years of age and before his ordination to the priesthood, what had been percolating in his mind, heart, and soul, coalesced into that great idea: the Militia Immaculata (MI), Mary's Army. The MI would be a spiritual army whose goal was to bring the whole world to Christ under the generalship of Mary.[115] The MI continues to this day to enlist countless members of all ages (seven years and older) and walks of life, from all over the world. Members consecrate themselves to Mary and join her in her Son's mission to save souls.

Maximilian taught that if we are under Mary's leadership and are obedient to her, we will be squarely in God's will. Going through Mary *in everything* ensures that we will stay the course intended by God. Maximilian tells us:

> Indeed, the very act of yielding yourself unreservedly to her will not only shows that you love the will of God, but also proclaims the truth that her will is so perfect that it deviates in nothing from the will of God.[116]

Basically, if you're with Mary, you can't go wrong.

---

[114] Treece, *A Man for Others*, 67.
[115] Marytown.com is a comprehensive website for the U.S. headquarters for the Militia Immaculata. It would be difficult to exhaust all the resources and information provided through Marytown, the National Shrine of St. Maximilian Kolbe.
[116] Fr. Anselm Romb, *Total Consecration to Mary: The Theology and History of Marian Consecration with a Nine-Day Preparation, in the Spirit of St. Maximilian Kolbe* (Libertyville, IL: Marytown Press, 2006), 53.

Rely on God to Get It Right

Almost Derailed

Like his spiritual father, Saint Francis of Assisi, Maximilian experienced a pivotal episode in his early life when he misinterpreted what the Lord was asking of him. It happened during his time in the minor seminary just after he and his older brother Francis had been notified of their acceptance into the novitiate. With the best of intentions and a sincere desire to do the will of God, Maximilian and Francis decided to leave the seminary and join the Polish military. When looking at it practically, it made sense. After all, Maximilian was multitalented and well suited for it (he had not contracted tuberculosis at this point). With his inventive mind and genius for strategy, his military service could prove quite substantial for his struggling country. At this juncture in his life, Maximilian had concluded that he would best serve God under Mary's leadership in the Polish military.

Just moments before he and Francis were to inform the prior of their decision to leave the Franciscans, someone came to the front door.

> How can I forget the moment when Francis and I, waiting
> for our appointment with Father Provincial to tell him we
> did not wish to enter the Order, heard the bell ring in the
> reception room. At that very delicate moment the God of
> providence, in his infinite mercy and through the services
> of Mary Immaculate, sent me my mother.[117]

We don't know what exactly transpired that day when the bell unexpectedly rang at the seminary door. But we do know that Mrs. Kolbe's boys did *not* keep their appointment with Father Provincial.

---

[117] Treece, *A Man for Others*, 10.

⁓

Reflection

A pure intention to do God's will with a reliance on the Blessed Mother provided the safety net for Maximilian to stay the course. It's no different for us. We can proceed with confidence trusting that God will take care of our missteps. St. Maximilian tells us:

> If even for a moment we were endowed with infinite intelligence and understood the cause and effect of everything, we would not choose for ourselves anything other than that which God allows, for he is infinitely wise and knows best. He wills and permits only that which will serve our greater happiness in heaven.... We can and must trust God. By such confidence, without immediately comprehending matters, we can give even greater glory to God.[118]

---

[118] Maximilian Kolbe, *Will to Love: Reflections for Daily Living*, compiled by Fr. George M. Domanski, O.F.M. Conv., eds. Brother Charles Madden, O.F.M. Conv., and Danile Gallio (Libertyville, IL: Marytown Press, 2013), 10.

☞

8

Trust the Lord Even When Things Don't Appear to Make Sense

*I am oppressed by the uncertainty of my future, but I
cherish the lively hope of seeing my dreams fulfilled,
because the Lord cannot place thoughts and desires in a
person's soul if He does not really intend to fulfill them,
to gratify these longings which He alone caused.*

—St. Pio of Pietrelcina

Saint Thérèse of Lisieux

Ambitious and conflicted: that was Thérèse of Lisieux—for a while. Her efforts to discern God's special mission were frustrating. She wanted to be everything for Jesus but could not accomplish some of the simplest tasks in daily life.

In her prayer to Jesus, we see that she struggles to figure out this mysterious incompatibility:

No doubt, those three privileges are my vocation—Carmelite, Bride, and Mother [of souls]—but I feel within myself other vocations. I feel the vocation of Warrior, Priest, Apostle, Teacher, Martyr. In short, I feel the need and the desire to accomplish for You, Jesus, all the most heroic works.... I feel in my soul the courage of a Crusader, of a soldier in the papal army; I would like to die on the field of battle for the defense of the Church....

I feel within me the vocation of Priest. With what love, Jesus, would I bear You in my hands when, at the sound of my voice, You would come down from Heaven.... With what love would I give You to souls![119]

Thérèse is honest with Jesus about her desires and dreams, which at face value are simply not achievable. She trusts that these desires must be from God and therefore there *must be* an answer for her. She continues:

Oh! In spite of my littleness, I would like to shed light on souls like the Prophets, the Doctors. I have the vocation to be an Apostle.... I would like to travel across the world, preach Your name, and plant Your glorious Cross on the soil of unbelievers. But, my Beloved, a single mission wouldn't be enough for me. I would at the same time like to preach the gospel in five parts of the world and as far as the remotest islands (Isa. 66:19).... I would like to be a missionary, not only for a few years, but I would like to have been one since the creation of the world and be one until the end of the age.... But above all, my Beloved Savior, I would like to shed my blood for You until the last drop.

She goes on about her desired martyrdom:

Like you, my Beloved Bridegroom, I would like to be scourged and crucified.... I would like to die by being

[119] Thérèse of Lisieux, *The Story of a Soul*, 170–171.

skinned alive like St. Bartholomew.... Like St. John, I
would like to be plunged into boiling oil. I would like to
undergo all the torture inflicted on the Martyrs.... With
St. Agnes and St. Cecilia, I would like to present my
neck to the sword, and like Joan of Arc, my dear sister,
I would like to be burned at the stake, murmuring your
name, Jesus.[120]

Thérèse continues on without inhibitions. She lays it all out
there for Jesus, even though what she suggests is not feasible.
And some points, such as having been a missionary from the
creation of the world, or becoming a priest, are utterly impossible. She bares her heart to Jesus, knowing that it does not make
sense. Then, with childlike simplicity, this young Carmelite puts
the question to Jesus:

To all my foolishness, what are You going to reply?...
Is there a soul that is smaller and more powerless than
mine?[121]

A Little Background

Thérèse Martin was born in Alençon, France, on January 2, 1873.
She was fortunate to grow up in a very pious and affectionate
family. Thérèse was the youngest, and her sisters doted on her.
In many ways Thérèse was spoiled. She was not expected to do
some of the basic tasks of daily life, such as house cleaning. Her
childhood, although idyllic in many ways, was not without hardship. Her mother died when she was four years old, and Thérèse
suffered terribly when her older sister Pauline (who had become

---

[120] Ibid., 171.
[121] Ibid., 171–172.

like a mother to her) left home to enter the Carmelite convent of Lisieux. Thérèse, however, did not lack the love and presence of her father: they were very close.

Thérèse received permission to enter the cloistered Carmelite convent of Lisieux at the age of fifteen, and just nine years later, she died of tuberculosis when she was only twenty-four years old. Hers was a short, obscure, and uneventful life. No one but her family, a few friends, and the nuns in the convent knew her.

With the exception of the Blessed Virgin Mary, how is it that Thérèse is arguably the most popular saint of all time?[122] This young Carmelite nun has a fiercely loyal worldwide following that can be explained only supernaturally.

Some people initially find it difficult to relate to or pray to this young saint who expressed herself in such flowery language. She can appear altogether too naive and sweet to handle anything a person in the twenty-first century might send her way. But when we dig a little deeper, we encounter a spiritual reality: to love (and therefore help) anyone is not predicated on having had similar experiences. Thérèse is tough; her loyal followers have found her to be the go-to saint for *any* ills we deal with in our modern world.

Thérèse's autobiography, *The Story of a Soul*, was published in 1898, one year after she died. By 1914, just sixteen years later, the Carmelite Convent at Lisieux where Thérèse had lived was receiving two hundred letters a day reporting miracles and stories attributed to her miraculous intercession. By 1923 the

---

[122] Ralph Martin, *Surrender to Love: The Wisdom of Thérèse of Lisieux* (Ann Arbor: Renewal Ministries, 2002), audio CD, disc 1, talk 1.

daily volume had increased to between eight hundred and one thousand letters.[123] Generally, supplicants receive roses or flowers letting them know that the Little Flower (the name for which she is affectionately known) is interceding for them. To this day, there is no shortage of testimonies of Saint Thérèse's involvement in the lives of those who seek her help.[124]

The Answer

The answer to Thérèse's conflicts—her pleading with Jesus, "To all my foolishness, what are You going to reply?"—was found in Scripture. She rightfully took it literally when she read, "But earnestly desire the higher gifts. And I will show you a still more excellent way" (1 Cor. 12:31). She continued reading and found the "more excellent way" in Saint Paul's discourse on love in chapter 13 of his first letter to the Corinthians.

> If I speak in the tongues of men and of angels, but have not love, I am a noisy gong or a clanging cymbal. And if I have prophetic powers, and understand all mysteries and all knowledge, and if I have all faith, so as to remove mountains, but have not love, I am nothing. If I give away all I have, and if I deliver my body to be burned, but have not love, I gain nothing.
>
> Love is patient and kind; love is not jealous or boastful; it is not arrogant or rude. Love does not insist on its own way; it is not irritable or resentful; it does not rejoice at wrong, but rejoices in the right. Love bears all things,

---

[123] Martin, *Surrender to Love*, disc 1, talk 1.

[124] Elizabeth Ficocelli, *Shower of Heavenly Roses: Stories of the Intercession of St. Thérèse of Lisieux* (New York: Crossroad Publishing Company, 2004).

believes all things, hopes all things, endures all things. (1 Cor. 13:1–7)

Her vocation was *love*. Now it all made sense! It is love that compels the missionary to travel to distant lands, leaving behind family, friends, and country. It is love that fortifies the martyr when spilling his blood for Christ. Love is what leads a man to the priesthood. Love for souls inspires the preacher to preach and the teacher to teach. Love transcends time because God is love and He is outside of time. Love can do all things.

Love is required in the Body of Christ, enabling the members to carry out their respective missions. Love is the glue of the Church. This was Thérèse's answer—delivered with the clarity and power of a lightning bolt. Thérèse would *be* the love that undergirds the priest, the missionary, the teacher, the doctor, the martyr, and the warrior. She would be *all things* for Jesus, through her participation in the Mystical Body of Christ.

The Little Way

Just how would Thérèse accomplish this in a practical way? For example, we might wonder how Saint Thérèse's love is used for the missionary or the priest? It sounds a bit abstract.

Although Thérèse got her answer, implementing it was another matter. Inspiration for her next move was inspired by the Old Testament figure Elisha and his daring request of Elijah.

Elijah said to Elisha, "Ask what I shall do for you, before I am taken from you." And Elisha said, "I pray you, let me inherit a double share of your spirit." (2 Kings 2:9)

So with the childlike audacity for which she is known, Thérèse presented herself to the angels and saints to make her bold appeal.

I am the littlest of creatures, I know my wretchedness and my weakness, but I also know how much noble and generous hearts love to do good. I beg you, then, you Blessed inhabitants of Heaven, I beg you to *adopt me as your child*. To you alone will be the glory that you will cause me to acquire, but deign to grant my prayer. It is foolhardy, I know, but nonetheless I dare to ask you to obtain this for me: *a double portion of your Love*.[125]

And what would she be able to do with a double portion of the love that had inspired all the saints since the dawn of Christianity? She was, after all, a cloistered nun who found it challenging enough to manage the daily duties of her life. In a prayer to Jesus, we see her strategy:

Yes, my beloved, that is how my life will be consumed.... I have no other means of proving my love for You than to throw flowers, that is, not to pass up any little sacrifice, any look, any word, to take advantage of all the little things and to do them out of love.... I want to suffer out of love and even rejoice out of love, so I will throw flowers before Your throne.[126]

The picture drawn by a child and given with love to her daddy is worth more to that father than an expensive masterpiece of art. Why? Because of the pure innocent love with which it was given. This is how Thérèse would throw flowers before the throne of Jesus. All the little things of her life (and the big things too when they came) would be offered to Jesus with her pure, childlike love.

---

[125] Saint Thérèse of Lisieux, *The Story of a Soul*, 175.
[126] Ibid., 176.

Thérèse did not have notable accomplishments to offer. Her seemingly insignificant sufferings, inconveniences, and embarrassments, no matter how small or unimportant, were what she had to give. So Thérèse was kind to the Sisters she found irritating. She did not complain about her food, even when she was served the worst leftovers. She did not defend herself when falsely accused or appeared incapable of a simple task. No one realized what she was doing or how much it cost her personally to suffer these secret humiliations. Thérèse's namesake, Blessed Mother Teresa, sums up beautifully this Little Way of Saint Thérèse: "Do ordinary things with extraordinary love."[127]

Loving God's Will above All
Thérèse preferred God's will to all else. Her union with Jesus was so great that she wanted *only* what He wanted. It is remarkable to think that many of the nuns in the convent were clueless as to her sanctity.[128]

God's will in our lives — our mission — sometimes is a very private affair. It may seem as if nothing supernatural is happening when spiritual battles are waged and souls are won for God, but He knows. What if our mission is to be a prayer warrior and spend much of our time interceding on behalf of others? That mission is not going to be obvious to others. And it is the same if God has asked us to unite our pains, sorrows, and trials with His Passion to save souls.

---

[127] Mother Teresa, *Where There Is Love, There Is God: A Path to Closer Union with God and Greater Love for Others*, ed. Brian Kolodiejchuk (New York: Image, 2012), 325.
[128] Her biological sisters did realize there was something special going on with Thérèse; her sister Pauline asked her to write her autobiography and write about her "little doctrine."

Thérèse suffered tremendously before dying of tuberculosis. She slowly suffocated for almost two months. Her limbs were swollen and purple; she spit up blood, perspired profusely, and eventually was unable to receive the Blessed Sacrament. She remarked that it was much more difficult than she had ever imagined. At the end, she would endure attacks from the devil.

> I don't know what cursed voice was saying to me, "Are you sure you are loved of God? Has He come to tell you so? It's not the opinion of a handful of people that will justify you before Him."[129]

How terrible it was to be tormented this way. One night Thérèse begged one of the Sisters to sprinkle holy water over her, saying, "The devil is around me. I can't see him, but I feel him."

Some of the Sisters would romanticize her impending death and suggest ideas such as, "Wouldn't it be nice if Thérèse received Communion and then died?" Thérèse would correct such suggestions by making sure that it was understood that she wanted only the will of Jesus. He would determine how she would die, and she would not ask that it be any other way, "I do not desire to die more than to live; it is what He does that I love."[130]

Spending Her Heaven on Earth

Before dying, Thérèse spoke these prophetic words:

> I feel that my mission is going to begin, my mission to cause the Good Lord to be loved as I love Him ... to give

---

[129] Saint Thérèse of Lisieux, *The Story of a Soul*, 254.

[130] Martin, *Surrender to Love*, disc 4, talk 4.

my little way to souls. I WANT TO SPEND MY HEAVEN DOING GOOD ON EARTH.[131]

And that is exactly what has happened. Earlier the question was posed, "With the exception of the Blessed Virgin Mary, how is it that Saint Thérèse is arguably the most popular saint of all time?"[132] She was virtually unknown by anyone but her family and the Carmelite nuns of Lisieux.

The Saint Thérèse phenomenon is proof that she is indeed spending her Heaven doing good on earth. And therefore her devotees, who have benefitted from her intercessions, are all too ready to share their personal stories and make an enthusiastic recommendation of her to any needy soul.

"The greatest saint of modern times" is what Pope Pius X called Thérèse. She was canonized in 1925 and two years later was declared co-patron of the missions with Francis Xavier. She was also declared co-patron of France with Joan of Arc, one of her favorite saints. Possibly most significant is her being declared the thirty-third Doctor of the Church by Pope John Paul II in 1997.

It's quite obvious that after passing from this world, Thérèse went right to work. Her mission, "to give my little way to souls," continues. We can and should solicit her help. After all, she told us she would not rest until "time is no more!"[133]

A Life-or-Death Quandary: Blessed Franz Jägerstätter

During World War II, Franz Jägerstätter sat in a Berlin prison. His crime — refusing to serve in the German infantry. Franz simply could not be complicit with the evil of Nazism.

---

[131] Saint Thérèse of Lisieux, *The Story of a Soul*, 261.
[132] Martin, *Surrender to Love*, disc 1, talk 1.
[133] Saint Thérèse of Lisieux, *The Story of a Soul*, 261.

Far from his home in Austria (which had been annexed to Germany), he awaited his trial and likely execution. While there, Franz received a welcomed visit from his wife, Franziska, and their local parish priest. The two had made the journey with one goal in mind: to convince Franz to relent and serve in the German army.

Pressure was brought to bear. Franziska presented her husband with a picture of his little daughters holding a sign that said, "Daddy, come home soon!" With the family being very close, loving, and affectionate, it was the best weapon she had. Franz adored his little girls. The photo must have been like a knife in his heart.

The parish priest obviously cared for the Jägerstätter family. One can imagine that he hoped to save the life of this beloved husband and father and to spare the family from the ensuing hardship they would face if he were executed. And Franz's courageous sacrifice would not make any perceptible difference — the Nazi war machine would continue on its unrelenting destructive path. The death of one insignificant Austrian farmer would go virtually unnoticed except for his loved ones left behind — who would undoubtedly suffer.

His bishop, as well as several other priests he had previously consulted, had already tried to persuade Franz to abandon his resolute stand. They had urged him to consider his station in life and his obligations to his family. To this he answered, "I cannot believe that just because one has a wife and children, he is free to offend God."[134] They encouraged him to obey the legitimate government and argued that it was the political authorities that

---

[134] "Bl. Franz Jägerstätter (1907–1943), Layman and Martyr," Vatican website, accessed October 2, 2015, http://wwwvatican. va/news_services/liturgy/saints/ns_lit_doc_20071026_ jagerstatter_en.html.

bore the responsibility for wrongdoing, not the law-abiding ordinary citizenry.[135]

> Everyone tells me, of course, that I should not do what I
> am doing because of the danger of death.... I believe it is
> better to sacrifice one's life right away than to place oneself in grave danger of committing sin and then dying.[136]

Cooperating with the government or not, Franz had good reason to believe he would not live to see peace restored. A staggering number of men from his region of Austria were being killed at the war front. If he were likely to die, he would rather do it for good than for evil.[137]

This humble Austrian was not a conscientious objector in the total sense. He had, in fact, been called up for military training and had willingly participated. But, over time, Franz began to realize and object to the evil of Nazism. When he returned from his training, he had made up his mind that if he were called again, he would refuse. He had, however, petitioned time and again to serve as a paramedic: a duty that this devout Catholic could perform in good conscience. Each time, however, his request was denied.

Growing in Holiness — A Preparation

In his teen years, Franz had associated with a rowdy crowd. He was the only one in the quaint village of Saint Radegund to own a motorcycle, and he had fathered a child out of wedlock.

---

[135] Robert Royal, *The Catholic Martyrs of the Twentieth Century* (New York: The Crossroad Publishing Company, 2000), 163.
[136] Ibid.
[137] O'Neel, *39 New Saints You Should Know*, 122.

But he was not without a conscience. Franz supported the child financially and fostered a relationship his little daughter.

With Franz's marriage to Franziska, things changed. She was a devout Catholic, and through her influence, Franz began to appreciate the Church. He was eager to know more about God and to grow in holiness. Franz took it upon himself to read the Bible, to perform spiritual works, and to learn about the Catholic Faith, including Church history.

Franz fasted each day until noon Mass, which was no little sacrifice, given the demands of farming. Although he and his wife made a meager living and had three little girls depending on them, the couple gave what alms they could to assist the poor in their village. Franz became a Third Order Franciscan. He also served his parish as the sacristan and never accepted the customary monetary offerings for weddings and funerals. He asked for prayers instead.[138]

A man of deep prayer and contemplation, Franz experienced a profound unity with the Lord that, according to the saints, is found in Heaven and rarely on earth. Before he was executed, Franz told Father Jochmann, the prison chaplain, "I am completely bound in inner union with the Lord."[139]

Rich in Faith
We hear these wise words from Franz:

> If a person were to possess all of this world's wisdom and be able to claim half of the earth as his own, he could and would still be less fortunate than a poor person who

---

[138] Ibid., 121.
[139] Royal, *The Catholic Martyrs of the Twentieth Century*, 165.

can claim nothing in this world as his own other than a deep Catholic Faith. I would not exchange my small dirty cell for a king's palace if I was required to give up even a small part of my faith. All that is earthly, no matter how much nor how beautiful, comes to an end. But God's word is eternal.[140]

Sometimes following God's will and embracing a particular mission that He has for us does not make worldly sense. Most can identify with Franz's wife and his parish priest who saw the sacrifice of this kind, good, and holy man as a waste — akin to throwing pearls before swine. He was taking a stand that the Church at that time did not ask of her members or openly support.[141] Socially and politically too, he was an enigma.

At his trial, even his accusers, who initially were arrogant in their superiority, became sympathetic. After hearing him, they did not want to execute the humble farmer from the little village in Austria. They, along with his lawyer, begged him to reconsider his position. Franz was resolute: "This regime is evil, and I cannot support it in any way."[142]

The prison chaplain, Father Jochmann, is the only one who fully supported Franz in his decision. He observed, "I can say

---

[140] *Franz Jägerstätter: A Man of Conscience*, directed by Jason A. Schmidt and Ron Schmidt (December 2nd Productions, 2010), DVD.

[141] With good reason. Public stands by the Church that were published during the time of the Nazi expansion, or secretly smuggled into churches to be read to the faithful, were met with massive and random executions. For a time, the Church was quiet in order to prevent even more bloodshed.

[142] O'Neel, *39 New Saints You Should Know*, 123.

with certainty that this simple man is the only saint I have ever met in my lifetime."[143]

On the day of his execution, this brave and humble man was calm, prayerful, and wholly united with the will of God. Franz Jägerstätter was beheaded on August 9, 1943.[144]

⌒

Reflection

When we distill our purpose down to the most essential thing, it is eternal life. We will live for an eternity in one place or another — Heaven or Hell. It is our human reality.

Franz Jägerstätter possessed an eternal perspective and complete trust in God. He knew what was most important and what was at stake, and he made his choice.

From prison he wrote to his wife and daughters.

Dearest wife,

I thank you once again from the bottom of my heart for everything you have done for me in my lifetime and for all the love you brought to me. Let us hope to meet again soon in heaven. Learn to become a family, loving one another and forgiving whatever may come....

Now, my dear children, when your mother reads you this letter, your father will already be dead. I would have gladly come to you, but the heavenly Father wanted it otherwise. Be well-behaved and obedient children. Pray

[143] Royal, *The Catholic Martyrs of the Twentieth Century*, 165.
[144] The Nazis sent their prisoners to the guillotine without blindfolds and face up. The execution of Edith Stein, Saint Teresa Benedicta of the Cross, O.C.D., had taken place exactly one year earlier at Auschwitz.

for your father so that we shall see each other soon in heaven.... I am completely bound in inner union with the Lord.[145]

[145] *Franz Jägerstätter: A Man of Conscience.*

9

*

Remember That God Has a Plan

However severe God's guidance may seem to us at times, it's always the guidance of a Father who is infinitely good, wise and kind. He leads us to our goal by different paths.

—Julie Billiart

Disconcerting Circumstances

With ourselves and in our families, our workplaces, and even our parishes, we all face struggles that come with being part of the human family. The unsavory circumstances we find ourselves in might be the result of our own sins or of our association with someone else (often a relative) and of which we are completely blameless. It's tempting to let these situations derail us from our mission — especially if they are embarrassing, stain our reputation, or make us feel contaminated. But in such cases, it is important to persevere in the spiritual life. *God has a plan.*

Saint Helena during the Roman Persecution

As a young woman, Helena looked forward to a promising future. She was the wife of Governor Constantius Chlorus.[146] Together

---

[146] Helena was contractually a common-law wife of Constantius.

they had a son named Constantine. Constantius Chlorus was a military tribune in one of Rome's smaller provinces, but he was ambitious, and when the opportunity presented itself, he cast Helena off to marry the stepdaughter of Maximian, the Western Augustus. This was no doubt a political move, as it resulted in his appointment as Maximian's Caesar.

It is likely that during this time Helena became a Christian. Rome was a dangerous place for a Christian to live. Labeled the scapegoat for Roman misfortunes, plagues, and financial woes, Christians suffered barbaric cruelties. If members of the minority Faith were found practicing their beliefs, they might be fed to starved wild animals as entertainment for the masses, or their bodies might be used as human torches to light the famous Appian Way.

The late third century and the early fourth century, during Helena's middle years, produced the worst of Christian persecutions under the Roman emperors Galerius and Diocletian. Public sacrifices to the imperial cult were mandatory. If Christians refused, they paid with their lives, often in the most excruciating and painful ways imaginable.

The Victory of the Cross

The Roman Empire was a divided kingdom governed by co-emperors, one of whom was Constantius Chlorus, who ruled the Western Kingdom. Upon his father's death, Constantine was proclaimed emperor of the West.[147] His plan was to unify the empire under his reign. The first step was to take Rome and with it the Eastern Empire, ruled by Maxentius, but Constantine was greatly outmatched by Maxentius's forces.

---

[147] *When Rome Ruled* (National Geographic, 2011), DVD.

Remember That God Has a Plan

On the eve of what was his most decisive engagement at the Milvian Bridge, Constantine was encamped with his men. Here the city of Rome, and with it the rule of the Eastern Empire, would be won or lost. Suddenly an unearthly sign appeared in the sky: a cross and on it the first two Greek letters of Christ's name, the Chi-Rho.

Seeing the sign, perhaps Constantine thought of his Christian mother, Helena. He must have recognized her teaching about Christianity in the image. *Could there be something to that belief of hers?* That night, Constantine had a dream in which Jesus Christ instructed him to put the Christian symbol on the helmets and shields of his soldiers. Without hesitation Constantine declared the Chi-Rho his new battle standard.

At the Milvian Bridge, Constantine drove Maxentius and his men into the Tiber River, where Maxentius, weighed down by his armor, drowned.

A New Era

As the new emperor, Constantine did what his citizens must have thought madness: he gave Christianity the full protection of Roman law. The mighty Roman Empire — Christian? It was inconceivable to any early-fourth-century Roman citizen. And yet a new era was dawning: not only was Christianity legal, but the emperor's mother was also a professed believer. Constantine had declared his mother "Augusta"; Helena was thereby venerated as empress and enjoyed a share of influence in Roman government,[148] which she no doubt used for the propagation of her Christian Faith.

---

[148] Carsten Peter Thiede and Matthew D'Ancona, *The Quest for the True Cross* (London: Orion Publishing Group, 2000), 30–31.

A Crisis for Helena

Constantine had four sons. Like his father, he put his first wife aside to marry a younger woman, Fausta. Through this union, three sons were born. But Constantine's eldest son, from his first marriage, Crispus, demonstrated the same military talent and leadership qualities as his father. Crispus was well loved by all, especially by his grandmother Helena. So it was surprising that Constantine one day had Crispus thrown into prison. Shortly afterward, and without a trial, he ordered the execution of Crispus.

Why this sudden and outrageous behavior? There are different stories about Fausta and Crispus. The most accepted explanation is that Fausta, rightly or wrongly, accused Crispus of raping her or doing something equally horrific.[149]

Some historians assume that Helena pleaded Crispus's innocence to Constantine. Could it be that Fausta wanted Crispus dead so her own sons would have primacy in the empire? How could Fausta's sons ascend to power if Crispus was in the way? In any case, Constantine promptly rescinded his deadly order, but it was too late. Crispus had already been executed in his prison cell.[150]

His next move was to deal with Fausta. Constantine ordered his wife's execution. She was put in a bath that was heated until she was dead.[151] By imperial decree, Crispus's and Fausta's names were removed from all histories and public records — as if these two people had never existed and these horrible events had never happened. Even to speak their names was strictly prohibited.

[149] *When Rome Ruled.*
[150] Ibid.
[151] Thiede and D'Ancona, *The Quest for the True Cross*, 29.

Given human nature, we can imagine that people must have shared the tantalizing information all the more, simply because it *was* forbidden. The news must have buzzed throughout the empire.

On a personal level, Helena's heart must have been broken. Not only did she lose her beloved grandson, but she also saw her only son commit murder twice, putting his soul in mortal danger. However, there was something else to consider, something more weighty for Helena to grieve over—the potential loss of Roman souls. The ruling family was in a particularly influential position regarding the propagation of the Faith, and *this* was their example. The elderly Helena did the only reasonable thing she could do—she sought the will of God.

The True Cross

Helena realized that if Christianity were to flourish, the people would need something substantial to rally behind. Indeed, the most significant relic in all of early Christendom—the True Cross of Christ—would certainly unite the people of the expansive Roman Empire through their common faith in Jesus Christ and fidelity to His Church. And so, with the full backing of Emperor Constantine, she set out on a royal pilgrimage to the Holy Land in search of the True Cross. This grand undertaking would two to four years to complete and would consume the last few years of the elderly Helena's life. She was in her late seventies, possibly in her early eighties—absolutely ancient for that era.

We know from Eusebius of Caesarea, a Roman bishop, historian, and theologian who died about A.D. 340, that the powerful Empress Helena Augusta was generous. He writes about Helena's pilgrimage to the Holy Land:

Especially abundant were the gifts she bestowed upon the naked and unprotected poor. To some she gave money, to others an ample supply of clothing; she liberated some from imprisonment, or from the bitter servitude of the mines; others she delivered from unjust oppression, and others again, she restored from exile.[152]

Using the credible writings of Eusebius about the location of our Lord's Crucifixion in conjunction with the oral traditions maintained by the faithful, Helena located Golgotha. The holy relic, the true Cross of Christ, was recovered. Portions of it were dispatched throughout the Roman Empire, but the majority of it remained in the Holy City of Jerusalem.

Helena traveled back to Rome in time to die; her son Constantine was at her bedside.

Who would have imagined things would turn out the way they did? Helena, born a commoner,[153] ended up becoming the most powerful woman in the world. It was through her less-than-ideal motherhood that she became Empress Helena Augusta. She had been a Christian during the great persecution, only to be later instrumental in Christianizing the entire Roman Empire. And, as a very old woman enduring the worst kind of personal tragedy and public humiliation, she suffered a blow that would have left most people broken and bitter. Saint Helena responded to the situation by turning to the Lord and embracing her unique mission.

---

[152] D'Ancona, *The Quest for the True Cross*, 41.

[153] Early Church writers refer to Helena as an innkeeper's maid, but her place of birth and parentage is not known for certain. Due to her lowly origins, Bishop Eustathius of Antioch snubbed her and her entourage as they traveled during their Holy pilgrimage to recover the Cross.

Remember That God Has a Plan

Sometimes the dysfunctional aspects of our lives, whether our own past or the behaviors of our close family members or associates, derail us from carrying out the mission God has for us. Saint Helena demonstrates that at *every stage of life*—no matter what our past, what happens, or how private or public the circumstances—the best course of action is to seek God's will and *do it anyway*.

The Mystic-Tailor: Servant of God Jan Tyranowski

Sometimes it seems as if we are not the right person for the job. We lack the necessary skills and temperament. But our shortcomings can serve us. They require us to rely on the Lord, and they keep us humble. When embracing the mission God has for us, humility and trust are the necessary ingredients.

How far-reaching will our particular mission be? What souls will be touched? We may not know until we reach Heaven. Such was the case of a rather unknown layman, Jan Tyranowski.

As priests were carted off by the Gestapo during the occupation of Poland in World War II, Jan Tyranowski, a tailor by trade, reluctantly stepped into unknown territory. He was asked to form and advise a group of young men, creating a youth ministry team for the young people of the parish. "Living Rosary" prayer groups were born from the undertaking. These groups, led by Tyranowski and his team members, provided the sorely needed spiritual, emotional, and practical support to young Poles through prayer, fellowship, and practicing the works of mercy.

At first glance, one might dismiss Jan Tyranowski, thinking the shy tailor would not be suited for youth ministry. In his rather reclusive lifestyle, he did not deal much with people. Jan was not at all attracted to the youth—the idea of speaking to them terrified him. Initially, they were wary of him as well; many of the young people of his parish thought he was peculiar.

Well, he *was* a mystic and that can qualify one as "peculiar." And he was rather eccentric and quite intense. But he was also devoted to the Virgin Mary and a student of Carmelite spirituality. Indeed, Jan possessed something very real and very needed—a connection with the Divine. This simple tailor was a gift from God to the Polish youth whose future was being torn from them by the Nazi war machine.

When Jan protested, he was told, "Do not be afraid, the Lord will help you."[154] The Lord blessed his efforts, and Jan was able clandestinely to bring together the team leaders and implement the Living Rosary groups that served as a lifeline for the young people suffering under the Nazi occupation.

Those involved had many close calls. Youth groups of any kind, especially those that promoted a Polish identity, of which Catholicism was central, were targeted by the Gestapo. Tyranowski's apartment was once raided during a Living Rosary gathering. We do not know what this soft-spoken man said to the Germans, but they left.

Jan continued to mentor his team of Living Rosary group leaders, adjusting his approach to suit each one personally. Karol Wojtyla, who would later become Pope John Paul II, was one of the team and a Living Rosary group leader. At this time, Karol was in his early twenties with not one living family member, and Jan Tyranowski helped fill the painful void. He was not only a

---

[154] Clare Anderson, "The Tailor-Mystic Who Inspired a Pope," *Faith* (March–April 2014), accessed February 13, 2015, http://www.faith.org.uk/article/march-april-2014-the tailor-mystic-who-inspired-a-pope.

mentor to young Karol but also a spiritual director, friend, and father figure. Karol blossomed under the guidance of the shy layman, soaking up all that Jan had to share. Later, as Pope John Paul II, he would say of Jan:

> He disclosed to me the riches of his inner life, of his mystical life.... In his words, in his spirituality and in the example of a life given to God alone, he represented a new world that I did not yet know. I saw the beauty of a soul opened up by grace.[155]

The number of young adults involved in the Living Rosary groups cannot be determined for certain; there were a few hundred at the most. But the simple tailor had a gift for nurturing souls. Out of those brave young people, eleven vocations were realized, Karol Wojtyla's among them.

Possibly Jan Tyranowski's most important God-given task at this particular time was his contribution to the spiritual formation of young Karol Wojtyla. We can follow this unlikely youth leader's influence all the way through John Paul's papacy. This simple mystic-tailor's yes to God is still bearing spiritual fruit today.

$\backsim$

Reflection

None of us knows to what extent our actions will impact others. John Paul II explains that because of the Incarnation, we are connected with *all* mankind, living and dead. Our actions go

---

[155] André Frossard and Pope John Paul II, *Be Not Afraid: Pope John Paul II Speaks Out on His Life, His Beliefs, and His Inspiring Vision for Humanity* (New York: St. Martin's Press, 1984), 18.

beyond space and time. Saying yes to God has a power beyond our imaginings, as Saint John Paul II tells us:

> Human acts go beyond their immediate surroundings and the social or political perimeter. Every human act passed through Jesus Christ and via him reaches others to the ends of the world.... By taking my human nature, he [Jesus] has put me in communication with the totality of the universe, visible and invisible, of the living and the dead, and the violence which I think I am committing in the shadows makes a distant unknown angel shudder. But the smallest merit acquired through this grace will *also* go to the most unprovided, who without knowing me awaits my good will, whether he is conscious or quite ignorant of this spiritual reversibility, which makes the poor man the permanent creditor of the rich. Since the Incarnation, human acts have infinite repercussions.[156]

---

[156] Frossard and Pope John Paul II, *Be Not Afraid*, 75.

10

☞

Be an Extraordinary Witness in Ordinary Life

You must understand now more clearly that God is calling you to serve him here and from the ordinary, material and secular activities of human life.

— Saint Josemaría Escrivá

Embracing the Cross: Blessed Roger Wrenno

Whatever mission God gives us, no matter how common it may appear, carries within it our potential sainthood. What God asks of us during our lifetime is the most appropriate and suitable means to our growth in holiness — whether our lives remain ordinary or take an extraordinary turn.

Sixteenth-century English weaver Roger Wrenno was a common man and a devout Catholic. His life probably would have been rather ordinary as a weaver and businessman if not for the dreadful persecutions of the Church during the English Reformation. Anyone found practicing the Catholic Faith was imprisoned and often executed. Many were offered acquittal if they would renounce their loyalty to the Catholic Church. The punishment for hiding a Catholic priest was death by hanging. The priests themselves were hunted down, hanged, drawn, disemboweled, and quartered. Their body parts were then fastened to prominent buildings and bridges.

Roger Wrenno was arrested for ministering to covert Catholics. In prison he met Father John Thules. These holy men never lost sight of their mission of evangelizing for the salvation of souls. Together, they converted four fellow inmates who were thieves and were also condemned to die.

Father Thules was hanged, disemboweled, and quartered. Roger Wrenno was sentenced to death by hanging, but it was no typical hanging. Something wondrous happened before he gave his final witness. The noose was placed around Roger's neck, but when he was hanged, the rope broke, and he fell to the ground, still alive and semiconscious. While waiting for the procurement of a new rope, Roger recuperated, regaining full consciousness. The new rope was delivered and prepared for the hanging. But before carrying out the final execution, the sheriff offered Roger a second chance to escape death if he would renounce his Faith. Roger responded by running to the scaffold ladder and eagerly scaling it. The sheriff asked, "Mr. Wrenno, why are you in such a hurry to die?" and Roger answered, telling the sheriff, "If you had seen that which I have just seen, you too would be eager to die."[157]

The Backdrop

Wherever the Catholic sun doth shine,
there's laughter and good red wine.
At least I've always found it so.
Benedicamus Domino.[158]

---

[157] *Faith of Our Father: In Search of the English Martyrs* (San Francisco: Ignatius Press, 2014), streaming video.
[158] "Benedicamus Domino" is Latin for "Let us bless the Lord."

Hilaire Belloc, who penned this verse, is ranked among England's greatest writers of the early twentieth century.[159] Long before it was accepted, Belloc argued that the English Reformation (in the sixteenth century), unlike the Protestant Reformation in other parts of Europe, was not a popular movement among the people. He asserted that the English Reformation was a political operation. Belloc was right.

Those in power, the reigning monarch or current government, control how history is recorded for posterity. Sometimes it can take centuries for the truth to be brought to light. This is mostly true regarding what has been generally believed about the English Reformation. However, upon an honest investigation, we find a people whose Catholic religion was torn from their culture in a systematic, calculated, and brutal way. It was done by the government—not through a movement born from the good English people.

The persecution of Catholics during the English Reformation saw many heroes. Some, such as Saint Thomas More, are well known, but there are many others to meet. A majority of our elder English brothers and sisters in the Faith were common folk with an uncommon love and commitment to Jesus Christ and His Church. They would not give up what they treasured most, and it cost them dearly.

Wife and Mother: Saint Margaret Clitherow

When the most rigorous of the Penal Acts in England was passed, Margaret Clitherow, a butcher's wife and mother of three, sought the advice of her spiritual director, Father John Mush. By this

---

[159] A devoted Catholic, Belloc was highly influential in the conversion of G. K. Chesterton.

time, punishment was as severe as it would get under Queen Elizabeth I. Anyone caught hiding a Catholic priest or celebrating the Holy Mass in their home would be arrested and hanged until dead.

Unbeknownst to her Protestant husband, John, this clandestine Catholic activity had been taking place regularly in the Clitherow home under Margaret's supervision. She and her children (in their teens by this time) were an active part of the underground movement that enabled Catholics secretly to attend Mass and receive the sacraments. This network of covert believers provided hiding places and escape routes for priests. Margaret asked Father Mush:

> May I not receive priests and serve God as I have done, notwithstanding these new laws, without my husband's consent?... I know not how the rigor of these new statutes may alter my duty to this thing: but if you tell me that I offend God in any point, I will not do it for all the world.[160]

Father Mush pointed out that for her husband's safety, it was best that he know as little as possible about the Catholic activity in the home. Her confessor reminded Margaret that her duty to God was above any law of the land and even the authority of her husband. And he also cautioned her that by obeying wicked laws, she would share in the guilt of those who enacted and carried out those laws.

Margaret was deeply devoted to her husband: "I love him next unto God in this world.... If I have offended my husband

---

[160] Margaret T. Monro, *St. Margaret Clitherow, "The Pearl of York"*: *Wife, Mother, Martyr for the Catholic Faith under Queen Elizabeth I* (Rockford, IL: TAN Books, 2003), 17.

in anything, but for my conscience [i.e., but for my religious duty], I ask God and him forgiveness."[161] God came first, of course, but her devotion and faithfulness to her husband and to her children were above reproach.[162] Remaining faithful to the Catholic Faith and teaching her children to do likewise was risky, but Margaret would not throw away eternity to gain security in the short term. "For what does it profit a man if he gains the whole world and loses or forfeits himself?"(Luke 9:25).

When Margaret had converted as a young unmarried woman, it was without reserve. She loved Jesus and His Church. She was Catholic to her core. Her husband, John, married her despite her religion. And although he would have liked her to join the Church of England, he respected her, and she him.

Margaret was strict with her children, but there was a beautiful balance in how she raised them. Cheerfulness and the sound of laughter were as much a part of the household as prayer and managing her husband's butcher shop. Despite the maltreatment, public tortures, and public executions that Catholics suffered under Elizabeth I, Margaret maintained a heartwarming demeanor. She had a great many friends and admirers. She was kind and pleasant to be around, and she never tired of performing works of mercy. With her husband's blessing and support, she provided for those in prison, who relied on the charity of others for their meals and material needs.

Margaret herself endured a few prison stays. These occurred intermittently over a fifteen-year period as the persecutions gained momentum and became more intense. Although the

---

[161] Ibid., 16.
[162] Both her sons became Catholic priests, and her daughter became a nun.

records are inconclusive, it is believed that she was pregnant during one internment[163] and probably allowed to go home to give birth. These jail terms afforded her the opportunity to pray, ponder, and make reparation for sin. She could not understand why other imprisoned Catholics did not see imprisonment as an opportunity and take spiritual advantage of the situation.[164]

Caring for her husband and family, supporting the persecuted Church, and loving her neighbor were all part of Margaret's spiritual formation. There was no division between her faithfulness to God and the normal things of life. Margaret made a telling comparison between nursing her babies and her willingness to shed her blood in martyrdom: "I confess death is fearful and the flesh frail, yet I mind by God's assistance to spend my blood in this Faith as willingly as ever I put my paps into my children's mouths."[165]

When the Clitherow home was searched and irrefutable evidence of the Catholic Mass found hidden (vestments, altar breads, and so forth), Margaret was arrested for the last time. She would never return home or be allowed to see her husband or children again. When she was brought before the judges, a great crowd gathered in the streets. Her friends and neighbors were openly weeping, her public hanging a certainty. This unashamedly Catholic woman was loved and respected in her community by Protestants and Catholics alike.

When accused, Margaret refused to enter a plea. By refusing, there would be no trial. Her children and friends would not be forced to testify, which would incriminate her, them, and others.

---

[163] Monro, *St. Margaret Clitherow*, 13.
[164] Ibid., 32.
[165] Ibid., 20.

Margaret was protecting those she loved. But that protection came with a price of "strong and hard punishment." Hanging was the execution of choice for the Catholics, but in this case, Margaret would be pressed to death.

Margaret's martyrdom occurred on Good Friday, March 25, 1586, by the old calendar that England was still following at the time.[166] That Margaret should pass through her own passion and death corresponding with the Lord's is not a likely coincidence. And although Margaret's date of birth cannot be absolutely ascertained, the evidence points to the real possibility that she was thirty-three years old, the age at which Christ is thought to have died. When being prepared for execution, she was ordered to lie on the floor, a sharp stone was placed beneath her back, and her hands were stretched out in the form of a cross and fastened down. A door was placed over her body and enormous weights were heaped upon it. Margaret died in about fifteen minutes. She had lived and died according to her intention:

> I am fully resolved in all things touching my Faith, which I ground upon Jesu[s] Christ, and by Him I steadfastly believe to be saved: which Faith I acknowledge to be the same that He left to His Apostles, and they to their successors from time to time, and is taught in the Catholic Church through all Christendom, and promised to remain

---

[166] Father John Morris, *The Catholics of York under Elizabeth* (London: Burns and Oates, 1891), digitalized by the Internet Archive, NOOK Study (2008), 265. England had not yet adopted the Gregorian calendar, as much of Europe had, but followed the old calendar. According to the Gregorian calendar, March 25 is the feast of the Annunciation, but according to the old calendar, it was Good Friday.

with her unto the world's end, and hell-gates shall not prevail against it; and by God's assistance I mean to live and die in the same Faith; for if an angel come from heaven, and preach any other doctrine than we have received, the Apostle biddeth us not believe him.[167]

The Faith of a Child

When children fix their hearts firmly on the Lord, their spiritual priorities become perfectly ordered. They see life with an uncomplicated purity. It is simple, holy, and quite impressive. Childlike faith is more challenging for adults, but Jesus tells us that it is the necessary goal.

> At that time the disciples came to Jesus, saying, "Who is the greatest in the kingdom of heaven?" And calling to him a child, he put him in the midst of them, and said, "Truly, I say to you, unless you turn and become like children, you will never enter the kingdom of heaven. Whoever humbles himself like this child, he is the greatest in the kingdom of heaven.
>
> "Whoever receives one such child in my name receives me; but whoever causes one of these little ones who believe in me to sin, it would be better for him to have a great millstone fastened round his neck and to be drowned in the depth of the sea." (Matt. 18:1–6)

When seeing heroic faith in a child, adults might ask, "How do they *get it* while still so young? Why don't they have to mature and go through the spiritual growing pains that are required of

---

[167] Monro, *St. Margaret Clitherow*, 8.

the rest of us?" Holiness does not require intelligence, chronological maturity, or a certain set of circumstances. God's grace is available to everyone, whatever their environment, even the young who often have little control over their lives.

An Ordinary Boy: José Sánchez del Río

Dear Mama,

I was taken prisoner during the fighting today. I think that now I am going to die. But that doesn't matter at all, Mama. Please accept God's will. I die very happy because I die on the battlefield right next to our Lord.

Don't let yourself be distraught by my death because that would only upset me more. Rather, tell my other brothers to follow the example of the littlest one, and you just do God's will. Be strong and please send me your blessing together with my Dad's.

Say goodbye to everyone for me one last time. And finally, accept all the love of your son who misses you so much already and wants to see you so much before he dies.

José[168]

By all appearances, José Sánchez del Río was an ordinary boy. He enjoyed the things that most boys do, such as hunting doves and playing games with friends — marbles were his favorite.[169] He also liked to ride and care for horses. José loved Jesus, served as an altar boy at Holy Mass, and prayed the Rosary every day.

---

[168] Cornelia R. Ferreira, *Blessed José Sánchez del Río* (Toronto: Canisius Books, 2006), 16. Blessed José Sánchez del Río wrote this letter from jail on February 6, 1928, when he was fourteen years old.

[169] O'Neel, *39 New Saints You Should Know*, 102.

The rhythms of the liturgical seasons determined the focus and activities for the families of Sahuayo, where José lived; a love for Christ and His Church as well as a tremendous devotion to Our Lady of Guadalupe permeated everyday life. It was through the normal home life of a family whose Catholic Faith was the priority that this Mexican boy grew in heroic faith.

The worst of the horrific Catholic persecutions in Mexico during the 1920s and '30s occurred during the four-year presidency (1924–1928) of Plutarco Elías Calles. It was under Calles that the Mexican government tried to wipe out Catholicism in the entire country. It was no small campaign: Church property was confiscated, and churches, Catholic schools, convents, and monasteries were shut down. There was torture and bloodshed beyond imagining. Priests were shot while offering Holy Mass. Lay and religious Mexican Catholics were shot, hanged, beaten, and often tortured; their bodies were displayed hanging from telephone poles.

The Cristero War was the people's response to the evil government, their battle cry: ¡Viva Cristo Rey! (Long live Christ the King!) José wanted to join the Cristeros like his older brothers, but his mother would not allow it. He persisted in his requests: "Mother, will you deny me a chance to go to heaven so soon?"[170] His grasp of the spiritual realities, the truth of the Faith that *she* had taught him, was firmly rooted in the heart of this loyal youth. For a whole year, José begged to be allowed to join the Cristeros. Finally, when he was just fourteen years of age, his mother tearfully relented.

---

[170] Christopher Check, "¡Viva Cristo Rey! The Cristeros versus the Mexican Revolution," *This Rock* 18, no. 7 (September 2007), posted at Catholic Answers, accessed October 3, 2015, http://www.catholic.com/magazine/articles/¡viva-cristo-rey.

Be an Extraordinary Witness in Ordinary Life

The commander in his hometown refused him. So the young but determined would-be Cristeros soldier traveled by horseback to the next town and presented himself to the commander there.

"What contribution can so small a boy make to our army?" The question was put to José.

"I ride well. I know how to tend horses, clean weapons and spurs, and how to fry beans and tortillas," was his confident answer.[171]

This time José was accepted. Before long he was promoted to bugler and standard-bearer. He would ride into battle alongside Cristeros commander Prudencio Mendoza.

All along, José seemed to realize he would be a martyr. He alluded to it from the very beginning when he argued for permission to join the Cristeros: "Mother, will you deny me a chance to go to heaven so soon?" Was his impending martyrdom apparent to the soldiers who were graced with his company? The youth had obviously made an impression on them — they nicknamed him Tarcisius after the young Roman martyr of the early Church who died protecting the Blessed Sacrament from a mob who attacked him as he carried the Sacrament to prisoners.

José would not die on the battlefield. Rather, he would be captured, tortured, and executed. During his captivity he was repeatedly promised his freedom in exchange for information about the Cristeros. He would not betray them or his Lord. "¡Viva Cristo Rey! ¡Viva Santa María de Guadalupe!" (Long live Christ the King! Long live Our Lady of Guadalupe!) was always his response.

The Federales, in an effort to break José's resolve, forced him to watch the hanging of a Cristeros soldier. As the brave man

---

[171] Ibid.

hung, suffocating, José offered encouragement, reminding him that they would soon see each other in Heaven. José was also forced to watch the hanging of his friend Lorenzo, an older youth who had served in the rebellion with him. Lorenzo's body was cut down and thrown aside. But he was not dead! Lorenzo escaped and rejoined the Cristeros.[172]

José suffered beatings, the flaying of the soles of his feet, several bayonet stabs, and a long grueling march on his soleless feet to his gravesite, where he was shot. During the gruesome ordeal, this courageous youth was repeatedly offered his freedom if he acquiesced to his executioners' demands. At the end, they tempted José further by telling him that he would live if only he would say, "Christ the King is dead." He remained faithful, responding, "¡Viva Cristo Rey! ¡Viva Santa Maria de Guadalupe!"

The Mission: the Will of God

Jesus' mission was to do the will of His Father—this was His task, His very sustenance. "My food is to do the will of him who sent me, and to accomplish his work" (John 4:34). During the Passion, Jesus reaffirmed His commitment to His Father's will: "Father, if thou art willing, remove this cup from me; nevertheless not my will, but thine, be done" (Luke 22:42).

José Sánchez del Río wanted the same thing as Christ. His mission was to do God's will. The letter he wrote to his mother as he awaited his execution clearly demonstrates this fact. First, he lovingly instructs her, "Please accept God's will." Then he asks his mother to remind his older siblings what is most important

---

[172] The older youth was aptly named Lorenzo, the Spanish version of Lazarus (see John 11:1–44).

of all: "tell my other brothers to follow the example of the littlest one, and ... just do God's will."

⌒

Reflection

Saint Josemaría Escrivá tells us:

> Everyday life is the true setting for your lives as Christians.
> Your ordinary contact with God takes place where your
> fellow men, your yearnings, your work and your affections
> are. There you have your daily encounter with Christ. It is
> in the midst of the most material things of the earth that
> we must sanctify ourselves, serving God and all mankind.[173]

Martyrdom will not be asked of most of us, but daily life provides the means for our growth in holiness. There are many opportunities to cooperate with God as he transforms us into saints. These opportunities might be as simple as answering a phone call from someone we would rather not deal with or choosing not to complain about something that irritates us. Other opportunities might be more difficult, such as losing a job or being rejected outright by a family member.

But for sure, the weavers, housewives, children, carpenters, bakers, farmers, and ranchers — the common, everyday Catholic people of the English Reformation and of the Mexican persecution of the twentieth century — grew in holiness through ordinary means. So, when the moment arrived, they were ready to give the ultimate witness rather than deny their Faith.

---

[173] Josemaría Escrivá, *In Love with the Church*, Josemaría Escrivá website, accessed October 3, 2015, http://www.escrivaworks. org/book/in_love_with_the_church-point-52.htm.

11

~

Meet the Guardian of Christ's Mission—and Yours Too

The Blessed Patriarch looks upon the multitude of Christians who make up the Church as confided specially to his trust—this limitless family spread over the earth, over which, because he is the spouse of Mary and the Father of Jesus Christ he holds, as it were, a paternal authority.

—Pope Leo XIII, *Quamquam Pluries*

Our Part in God's Plan

There's no doubt that the greatest mission, the one with the most hanging in the balance—at least as far as all of mankind is concerned—is Jesus' work of redemption. And it is wholly through Jesus Christ, the God-Man, that mankind is saved. The Lord in His great wisdom, however, involves others in the mystery of salvation.

God does not need anything; He is complete in Himself. But in His wisdom He became one of us—fully embracing His human nature with all its vulnerabilities and needs. The Virgin Mary's consent and participation was necessary for Jesus to carry out His mission. The same can be said for Saint Joseph.

Discover Your Next Mission from God

John Paul II explains this in his apostolic exhortation *Redemptoris Custos*:

> [Christ's] redemptive plan, which is founded on the mystery of the Incarnation ... in which Joseph of Nazareth "shared" like no other human being except Mary, the Mother of the Incarnate Word. He shared in it with her; he was involved in the same salvific event; he was the guardian of the same love, through the power of which the eternal Father "destined us to be his sons through Jesus Christ" (Eph 1:5).[174]

When it comes to our particular mission from God, we can count on the powerful intercession, guidance, protection, and provision of Saint Joseph. On earth, Joseph was a man of action. From Heaven, he still is.

"Saint Joseph's Little Dog": Saint André Bessette

A young mechanic who worked in a factory was holding a bowl of molten lead when it unexpectedly exploded in his face. In 1925 he wrote a letter testifying to the advice given to him by Brother André Bessette. Here is an excerpt:

> Finally the good Brother André showed up at the end of the hallway, and asked what was going on. I said to him, "Brother André, as you can see, I'm much too young to lose my eyesight.... You surely can do something for me." Brother André answered, and I'm writing down the exact words of his reply, "Who says you're going to lose your

[174] John Paul II, *Redemptoris Custos: On the Person and Mission of Saint Joseph in the Life of Christ and the Church*, August 15, 1989, no. 1.

eyesight? You have faith in Saint Joseph? Well then, go to church, attend Mass, and receive Holy Communion in honor of Saint Joseph. Keep on taking your medication, add to it a drop of Saint Joseph's oil, and make the following invocation, 'Saint Joseph, pray for us.' All will go well. Good day! Have faith."

I did exactly as I had been told.... To sum up, let me just say this: the same evening, my fiancée applied my medication with some of the oil, and we recited the invocation in honor of Saint Joseph. The next day — oh! How wonderful! — the scars on my face peeled away like sheets of cellophane paper. My eyelids were completely healed. My face was as fine as could be. No scars left, no pain whatsoever.[175]

Unimpressive to behold, uneducated, often sick, and very small (standing only five feet tall), Brother André appeared to be an unlikely person to dispense spiritual counsel to others or secure their healing from the Lord. The tasks given to him by the Congregation of the Holy Cross were the lowliest. He washed floors, served as doorkeeper, retrieved the mail, rang the Matins bell, worked in the laundry, and performed other menial jobs. It was in his role as doorkeeper and his brief personal encounters with those he welcomed to Notre Dame College in Montreal that his holiness became apparent.

Brother André believed that it was his task to propagate the devotion to Saint Joseph. It seems that the Holy Patriarch was in agreement; Saint Joseph readily answered Brother André's

---

[175] Jean-Guy Dubuc, *Brother André: Friend of the Suffering, Apostle of Saint Joseph* (Notre Dame, IN: Ave Maria Press, 2010), 106–107.

requests. Saint Joseph and Brother André were an inseparable team, bringing the needs of hurting people to Jesus for healing. The fruit produced through this friendship was astounding. (This is what it is to access the Communion of Saints—we work in tandem with the saints in Heaven as we carry out the mission God has assigned to us). Because of his role in the Holy Family and his cooperation in the plan of salvation, Saint Joseph has primacy (second only to the Virgin Mary) in the Communion of Saints. Blessed Pope Pius IX clarified this for us:

> Because of the sublime dignity which God conferred on his most faithful servant, the Church has always most highly honored and praised blessed Joseph next to his spouse, the Virgin Mother of God, and has besought his intercession.[176]

For the twenty-seven years leading up to Brother André's death in 1937, an estimated ten thousand people received healing—all of which Brother André attributed to the good Saint Joseph's intercession.[177] Often Brother André was given credit as the healer, but he continually set the record straight: "I do not cure; Saint Joseph cures." In fact, the humble Holy Cross monk considered himself to be nothing more than "Saint Joseph's little dog."[178]

Other saints have testified to Saint Joseph's sure assistance. Saint Teresa of Ávila was continually amazed at his involvement in her life:

---

[176] Mark Miravalle, *Meet Your Spiritual Father: A Brief Introduction to St. Joseph* (Sycamore, IL: Lighthouse Catholic Media and Marian Press, 2015), 72.

[177] Bert Ghezzi, *Voices of the Saints: A Year of Readings* (New York: Doubleday, 2000), 31.

[178] Dubuc, *Brother André*, 114.

I took for my advocate and lord the glorious St. Joseph and earnestly recommended myself to him. I saw clearly that as in this need so in other greater ones concerning honor and loss of soul, this father and lord of mine came to my rescue in better ways than I knew how to ask for. I don't recall up to this day ever having petitioned him for anything that he failed to grant. It is an amazing thing the great many favors God has granted me through the mediation of this blessed saint, the dangers I was freed from both of body and soul.[179]

Teresa of Ávila understood Joseph's privileged position in the Holy Family and in the Communion of Saints. And because she is a Doctor of the Church (as well as a saint) we can rely on her insights and teachings:

The Lord wants us to understand that just as He was subject to St. Joseph on earth—for since bearing the title of father, being the Lord's tutor, Joseph could give the Child command—so in heaven God does whatever he commands.[180]

Like Brother André, Teresa simply could not keep this good news to herself; she was compelled to share the benefits of friendship with Saint Joseph. She wanted everyone to know about this most magnanimous saint and spiritual father. Teresa challenged those she advised to "try" (or, in some translations of her

---

[179] Teresa of Ávila, *The Book of Her Life*, trans. Kieran Kavanaugh, O.C.D. and Otilio Rodriguez, O.C.D. (Indianapolis: Hackett Publishing, 2008), 27.

[180] Ibid., 27–28.

autobiography, "test") Saint Joseph. There were no doubts in her heart — Saint Joseph would come through for them.

> Because of my impressive experience of the good this glorious saint obtains from God, I had the desire to persuade all to be devoted to him. I have not known anyone truly devoted to him and rendering him special services who has not advanced more in virtue. For in a powerful way he benefits souls who recommend themselves to him.
>
> This has been observed by other persons, also through experience, whom I have told to recommend themselves to him. And so there are many who experiencing this truth renew their devotion to him.
>
> I only ask for the love of God those who do not believe me to try, and they will see through experience the great good that comes from recommending oneself to this glorious patriarch and being devoted to him.[181]

Saint Faustina too, benefited from the paternal guidance of Saint Joseph:

> Saint Joseph urged me to have a constant devotion to him. He himself told me to recite three prayers [the Our Father, Hail Mary, and Glory Be] and the Memorare[182] every day. He looked at me with great kindness and gave me to know how much he is supporting this work [of mercy]. He has promised me this special help and protection. I recite the requested prayers every day and feel his special protection. (*Diary*, no. 1203)

---

[181] Teresa of Ávila, *The Book of Her Life*, 28.
[182] This prayer appears in this chapter's "Reflection."

Meet the Guardian of Christ's Mission

Guardian of the Mystery of God

God "entrusted His greatest and most precious treasures"[183] to Joseph, "Guardian of the Mystery of God."[184] Jesus and Mary were dependent on Saint Joseph's protection and provision. In this way, Joseph of Nazareth was the custodian of Christ's mission. Whether it is realized or not, all mankind, past, present, and future, relies on Joseph. We owe Saint Joseph our heartfelt gratitude! His cooperation in the plan of salvation made Christ's redemptive work possible. Saint John Paul II said:

> I am convinced that by reflection upon the way that Mary's spouse shared in the divine mystery ... the whole Christian people not only will turn to St. Joseph with greater fervor and invoke his patronage with trust, but also will always keep before their eyes his humble, mature way of serving and of "taking part" in the plan of salvation.[185]

Despite all the uncertainties surrounding Mary's pregnancy, Joseph's focus was not on himself or his challenging situation but on doing the will of God. This humble carpenter, the "just man," as Saint Matthew describes him in his Gospel (1:19), never hesitated to do what the Lord asked of him. Pope John Paul II explains:

> "When Joseph woke from sleep, he did as the angel of the Lord commanded him and took Mary as his wife" (Mt 1:24). He took her in all the mystery of her motherhood.

---

[183] John Paul II, *Redemptoris Custos*, no. 32.
[184] Ibid., no. 5.
[185] Ibid., no. 1.

He took her together with the Son who had come into the world by the power of the Holy Spirit. In this way he showed a readiness of will like Mary's with regard to what God asked of him through the angel.[186]

Joseph supported his young wife as she carried the Incarnate Son of God in her womb and during the uncertainties surrounding the Christ Child's birth. The faithful and chaste husband of Mary continually protected and provided for the Holy Family.

Joseph named Jesus, giving his adopted son claim to the line of King David. Through his prompt obedient action, Joseph protected Jesus from the deadly intentions of King Herod. During their travels and exile, Joseph kept the child Jesus and His Mother, Mary, safe.

As the head of the Holy Family, Joseph was in authority over Jesus. Jesus was subject to Joseph as a son is to a father because Joseph *is* the virginal father of Jesus[187] — not in the biological sense but in all the ways that make a man truly a father. Saint Luke writes of both Mary and Joseph as Jesus' "parents." And when Mary addresses her Son, she refers to Joseph as His father.

And when they saw him they were astonished; and his mother said to him, "Son, why have you treated us so? Behold, your father and I have been looking for you anxiously." (Luke 2:48)

Because of our relationship with Jesus, Joseph is also our spiritual father. In fact, the Church formally entrusted us to his

---

[186] John Paul II, *Redemptoris Custos*, no. 3.
[187] Miravalle, *Meet Your Spiritual Father*, chap. 6.

paternal care and protection by declaring Saint Joseph Patron of the Universal Church.[188]

Guidance from Pope Francis

It's no secret that Pope Francis is devoted to the holy patriarch. He keeps a statue of the sleeping Saint Joseph on his desk and slips prayer intentions beneath it.[189] And the pope recommends us to Joseph. He explains how Joseph was able to perceive and embrace his mission from God (which continues from Heaven). Pope Francis knows that in Saint Joseph "we learn how to respond to God's call."

> How does Joseph respond to his calling to be the protector of Mary, Jesus and the Church? By being constantly attentive to God, open to the signs of God's presence and receptive to God's plans, and not simply to his own.... Joseph is a "protector" because he is able to hear God's voice and be guided by his will; and for this reason he is all the more sensitive to the persons entrusted to his safekeeping. He can look at things realistically; he is in touch with his surroundings; he can make truly wise decisions. In him, dear friends, we learn how to respond to God's call, readily and willingly, but we also see the core of the Christian vocation, which is Christ![190]

---

[188] Ibid., quoting Blessed Pius IX, *Quemadmodum Deus*.

[189] "The Statue of St. Joseph That Pope Francis Keeps in His Room," Rome Reports, March 19, 2015, accessed October 3, 2015, http://www.romereports.com/pg160745-the-statue-of-st-joseph-that-pope-francis-keeps-in-his-room-en.

[190] Pope Francis, Homily for the Inaugural Mass of Petrine Ministry, March 19, 2013, News.VA, accessed October 3, 2015,

Like Saint Joseph, once we have heard God's voice, we must rise from our slumber. We must get up and act![191]

☞

Reflection

If we hope to discern and embrace God's will in our lives, we need to do it Joseph's way—being attentive to the Lord and responding to Him in humble obedience. That is easier said than done. But no worries—our spiritual father, Saint Joseph is there to help us.

Saint Faustina's religious community prayed this version of the Memorare to Saint Joseph every day.

Memorare to Saint Joseph

Remember, O most pure spouse of Mary, and my dearly beloved guardian, Saint Joseph, that never was it known that anyone who invoked your care and requested your help was left without consolation. Inspired with this confidence, I come to you and with all the ardor of my spirit I commend myself to you. Do not reject my prayer, O Foster Father of the Savior, but graciously receive and answer it. Amen[192]

---

http://www.news.va/en/news/pope-homily-for-inaugural-mass-of-petrine-ministry.

[191] "Pope Francis to Families: Be Examples of Holiness, Prayer," meeting with families on January 16, 2015, in the Philippines, Vatican Radio, accessed October 3, 2015, http://en.radiovaticana.va/news/2015/01/16/pope_francis_to_families_be_examples_of_holiness,_prayer/1118503.

[192] Miravalle, *Meet Your Spiritual Father*, 141.

12

*

Follow Your Blessed Mother's Instructions

The love of the Father and Son and Spirit burns eternally. The love of the Father, of Jesus, and of the Immaculata (Immaculate Mary) knows no impairment in itself.... Hence, we must kindle this love about ourselves once it has been set afire in our own hearts. We must kindle the hearts of each and every one of those who are and of those who will be. We must light that glowing fire in ourselves and in the whole world, light it that it may emit greater and greater warmth without limit — such is our goal.

— Saint Maximilian Kolbe, *Will to Love*

A Marian Pope: Saint John Paul II

A person going on a trip into unknown territory will usually enlist the help of an experienced guide. So when discerning a mission given to us by God and *doing it* — a quest with eternal consequences — we certainly ought to have a qualified guide, and there is none better than the Blessed Mother. Mary is the best partner we can have on our quest, and there's a bonus: she will also be working on *her* current mission,[193] which is to form us into saints. It's a win-win situation.

[193] *Lumen Gentium*, no. 62.

Saint Pope John Paul II followed our Lord's example by entrusting himself to Mary. "Totus Tuus" (totally yours) was John Paul II's motto. If Jesus depended on and trusted the Blessed Mother when He was most vulnerable (in the womb and as a child growing up in Palestine), John Paul II could trust her with his life as well. And he did—completely.

Before Karol Wojtyla saw his twenty-first birthday, he had lost everyone he loved. A sister was born before him who had not lived past infancy. Karol's mother had died when he was just nine years old. His older brother, Edmund, whom Karol absolutely adored, died three and a half years later. For the Wojtyla family, it was just Karol and his father left to face the Nazi occupation of Poland that began in 1939.

He and his father, the elder Karol Wojtyla, were very close and shared a modest apartment in Kraków. At this time, during the occupation, Karol was a factory worker. One day, when he and a friend returned home after a shift, they entered the flat and discovered the lifeless body of Karol's father. The broken young man stayed with his father's body all through the night. His soul was in anguish, and he cried, "I'm all alone.... At twenty I've already lost all the people I've loved!"[194]

But he would lose more to the Nazi war machine. Friends, priests, and fellow seminarians would be taken to death camps, their lives extinguished in one horrific way or another. Loss—great heart-wrenching loss—was intertwined in this man's formation. Karol Wojtyla endured hard labor in the quarry, had several close calls with death, and engaged in risky underground movements: the Polish theater, Living Rosary youth groups, and eventually,

---

[194] Peggy Noonan, *John Paul the Great: Remembering a Spiritual Father* (New York: Penguin, 2005), 130.

the seminary. These activities would have almost anyone constantly on edge, rubbing one's nerves raw.

We all know people, ourselves included, who have suffered far less and yet remain deeply damaged because of it. Hardship, cruelty, and injury take a toll on us. The effects can inhibit our relationships, make it more difficult to love and trust, and disrupt how we develop physically, mentally, emotionally, and even spiritually. Sometimes we just don't function very well when it comes to basic things, such as holding down a job or remaining faithful to our obligations.

So how is it that Karol Wojtyla wasn't wounded to a dysfunctional point? One would think he would have been broken or hardened and would lack joy after all he suffered. But it was quite the contrary. For his entire life, John Paul II retained and continued to develop a tremendous capacity to love. His remarkable intellect served him throughout his life. And there are few people who have had more positive influence on the entire world. What, or rather, *who* made the difference?

There was a definitive moment of grace in the life of Karol Wojtyla as a young adult. This tremendous life-impacting gift came from a little book, *True Devotion to the Blessed Virgin*, by Saint Louis de Montfort, a priest and Third Order Dominican. John Paul II explains what happened:

> The reading of this book was a decisive turning-point in my life ... which coincided with my clandestine preparation for the priesthood. It was at that time that this curious treatise came into my hands.... I remember carrying it on me for a long time, even at the sodium factory.... I continually went back to certain passages....
>
> As a result, my devotion to the Mother of Christ in my childhood and adolescence yielded to a new attitude

springing from the depths of my faith, as though from the very heart of the Trinity and Jesus Christ.

What is more, this "perfect devotion" is indispensable to anyone who means to give himself without reserve to Christ and to the work of redemption.[195]

A true devotion to the Blessed Virgin Mary was essential to John Paul II as he carried out the multiple missions that God continually put before him. Mary guided him, mothered him, befriended him, and led him deep into the mysteries of the Trinity. He even credited her with saving his life. Because of Mary's unique relationship with each person of the Holy Trinity, she is specifically qualified for these tasks. Mary of Nazareth is the obedient Daughter of God the Father, the Spouse of the Holy Spirit, and the Mother of Jesus. And for John Paul II, she is the one who made all the difference.

God's Example

Jesus' mission, to save humanity through His life, death, and Resurrection, is the greatest gift any of us could ever receive. Because of Jesus, our broken relationship with God is restored: we are incorporated into the Body of Christ and adopted into the family of God.

The great mission to redeem mankind began with trust. God trusted Mary by first commending Himself to her at the Incarnation. John Paul II explains:

For it must be recognized that before anyone else it was God himself, the Eternal Father, who entrusted himself

---

[195] Frossard and Pope John Paul II, *Be Not Afraid*, 125.

to the Virgin of Nazareth, giving her his own Son in the mystery of the Incarnation.[196]

The Holy Virgin of Nazareth has been involved in Christ's work of salvation ever since,[197] and her irreplaceable participation will continue until the end of time. Jesus does the saving: being fully God and fully man, He is the only one who can. But by His divine design, the whole plan was subject to, and dependent on, Mary.

The Council Fathers of Vatican II shed light on the Virgin Mary's unique motherly participation with her Son Jesus on our behalf:

> She conceived, gave birth to, and nourished Christ, she presented him to the Father in the temple, shared his sufferings as he died on the cross. Thus, in a very special way she cooperated by her obedience, faith, hope and burning charity in the work of the Savior in restoring supernatural life to souls. For this reason she is a mother to us in the order of grace.
>
> This motherhood of Mary in the order of grace continues without interruption from the consent which she loyally gave at the Annunciation and which she sustained without wavering beneath the cross, until the eternal consummation of all the elect. Taken up to heaven, she did not lay aside this saving office but by her manifold intercession continues to procure for us the gifts of eternal

---

[196] John Paul II, *Redemptoris Mater*, March 25, 1987, no. 39.

[197] *Lumen Gentium*, no. 57. "This union of the mother with the Son in the work of salvation is made manifest from the time of Christ's virginal conception up to his death."

salvation. By her motherly love she cares for her Son's sisters and brothers who still journey on earth surrounded by dangers and difficulties, until they are led into their blessed home.[198]

Some will continue to criticize the Catholic acknowledgment of Mary's participation in the plan of salvation. But God *did* involve her. Mary is essential to Christ's mission. Why God designed it this way is a beautiful mystery. We can be sure that He has His reasons:

> For my thoughts are not your thoughts, neither are your ways my ways, says the Lord. For as the heavens are higher than the earth, so are my ways higher than your ways and my thoughts than your thoughts. (Isa. 55:8–9)

The Gift

"When Jesus saw his mother, and the disciple whom he loved standing near, he said to his mother, 'Woman, behold, your son!' Then he said to the disciple, 'Behold, your mother!' And from that hour the disciple took her to his own home" (John 19:26–27).

Jesus gave us His Mother. Mary's motherhood to us is a major component of her mission; it is all a part of God's plan. Bishop Fulton Sheen explains:

> Here is the answer ... to the mysterious words in the Gospel of the Incarnation which stated that Our Blessed Mother laid her "firstborn" in the manger. Did that mean that Our Blessed Mother was to have other children? It certainly did, but not according to the flesh. Our Divine

---

[198] *Lumen Gentium*, nos. 61–62.

Lord and Savior Jesus Christ was the unique Son of Our Blessed Mother by the flesh. But Our Lady was to have other children, not according to the flesh, but according to the spirit![199]

As a spiritual Mother, she continues to bring forth children into the Mystical Body of Christ—the Church. We are those spiritual children. With our permission and cooperation, Mary helps us grow in holiness and become saints so we can one day say, like Saint Paul, "it is no longer I who live, but Christ who lives in me" (Gal. 2:20). And, if that isn't amazing enough, this relationship with our heavenly Mother is personal to each one of us. John Paul II explains:

> Motherhood always establishes a unique and unrepeatable relationship between two people: between mother and child and between child and mother. Even when the same woman is the mother of many children, her personal relationship with each one of them is of the very essence of motherhood. For each child is generated in a unique and unrepeatable way.[200]

What we believe and how we respond does not change *what is*. The profound reality for all humanity is that Mary is our Mother. The Blessed Mother doesn't just love all her children in a general way: she knows and loves us each individually, tenderly, and maternally. See her love, her tone, her caring in her message to Saint Juan Diego. Her words are for us too.

---

[199] Fulton J Sheen, *The Life of Christ: The Seven Words from the Cross* (New York: McGraw-Hill, 1958), 396–397.

[200] John Paul II, *Redemptoris Mater; On the Blessed Virgin Mary in the life of the Pilgrim Church*, March 1987, no. 45.

Listen and let it penetrate your heart, do not be troubled
or weighed down with grief. Do not fear any illness or
vexation, anxiety or pain. Am I not here who am your
Mother? Are you not under my shadow and protection?
Am I not your fountain of life? Are you not in the folds of
my mantle? In the crossing of my arms? Is there anything
else you need?[201]

Mary pondered mysteries in her life. We too could ponder
each line she spoke to Saint Juan Diego and continually find
spiritual treasure in them.

Mary's Response and Ours

Discerning God's will for us will likely come with plenty of uncertainties. We might be tempted to think, *I will pray and discern
further until I know the whole plan.* But let's look at the Virgin
Mary and see how she responded to the portion revealed to her,
along with the accompanying boatload of unknowns.

When Mary said yes to God at the Annunciation—"Behold,
I am the handmaid of the Lord; let it be to me according to
your word" (Luke 1:38)—she did not know the entire design.
As a matter of fact, she knew very little about her future. That
specific lack of knowledge did not stop her from responding and
embracing God's special plan for her.

The angel Gabriel told her, "And behold, your kinswoman
Elizabeth in her old age has also conceived a son; and this is
the sixth month with her who was called barren" (Luke 1:36).
And she responded: "In those days Mary arose and went with

---

[201] John LaBriola, *Onward Catholic Soldier: Spiritual Warfare according to Scripture, the Church and the Saints* (Orange, CA: Luke
1:38 Publishing, 2008), 9–10.

haste into the hill country, to a city of Judah, and she entered the house of Zechariah and greeted Elizabeth" (Luke 1:39–40). Once Mary knew her current mission, in this case to go to her cousin Elizabeth, she did it immediately. She did not procrastinate. She did not wait to know God's entire plan. Rather, Mary "went with haste."

We cannot hear, see, or perceive as clearly as the Blessed Mother did. Her human nature was never damaged by sin, and she is therefore "full of grace." We, on the other hand, must put our ideas and inspirations through a careful discernment process to determine whether what we are considering is actually from the Lord. This may involve a fair amount of prayer and study. It often includes the wisdom and spiritual insights of others, such as a spiritual director or friends whose judgments we trust. Enlisting the prayers of the saints on our behalf is always a benefit. Sometimes we are required to wait on the Lord's answer as we continue discerning and pondering our particular situation.

But, when we do *finally* discern something that God is showing us, we need to get to it, just as Mary did. Our yes to what has been properly discerned, even if it's only a small part, is very likely necessary to the entire mission — even when we do not know the whole plan.

God sometimes will show us where we will go, but not all the steps to get there. Or He might reveal the first things He wants us to do, while the end remains hidden. We might not be ready to consider steps 2 and 3 until we have completed step 1. Or it could be that we first must pass through a time of testing. The revelation of the mission to us is God's doing, not ours. He will disclose what we need to know when we are ready.

We know that "Mary kept all these things, pondering them in her heart" (Luke 2:19). She devoted her attention to the things God revealed in her life. We can ponder the same things that Mary did. Actually, we do just that when we meditate on the Mysteries of the Rosary. And like our Blessed Mother, we should also reflect on our own experiences, pondering what God is working on in our lives.

Personal Experiences from the Communion of Saints

It would be difficult to find someone with a bigger heart for others than Blessed Mother Teresa. But this faithful servant of Jesus, who sought to satiate her Savior's thirst on the Cross by serving the poorest of the poor, often made this request of the Blessed Mother: "Lend me your heart."[202] That's how she loved and served so beautifully — with Mary's heart!

Saint Faustina Kowalska's vocation was precious to her. She therefore entrusted her perpetual vows to the Blessed Mother (*Diary*, no. 260). Mary guided Faustina, instructing her with motherly love:

> I desire, My dear beloved daughter, that you practice the three virtues that are dearest to Me — and most pleasing to God. The first is humility, humility, and once again humility; the second virtue, purity; the third virtue, love of God. As My daughter, you must especially radiate with these virtues. (*Diary*, no. 1415)

And like Mother Teresa, Faustina also received a portion of Mary's heart. Faustina tells us what happened after a visit from the Blessed Mother:

---

[202] Michael E. Gaitley, *33 Days to Morning Glory: A Do-It-Yourself Retreat in Preparation for Marian Consecration* (Stockbridge, MA: Marian Press, 2012), 75.

When the conversation ended, She pressed me to Her Heart and disappeared. When I regained the use of my senses, my heart became so wonderfully attracted to these virtues; and I practiced them faithfully. They are as though engraved in my heart. (*Diary*, no. 1415)

Young Father Fulton Sheen wanted to safeguard his vocation. And who better to turn to than the Mother of Jesus — the perfect and most faithful disciple? On the day of his ordination to the priesthood, he made the following commitment:

I would offer the Holy Eucharist every Saturday in honor of the Blessed Mother to solicit her protection on my priesthood. The Epistle to the Hebrews bids the priest offer sacrifices not only for others, but also for himself, since his sins are greater because of the dignity of the office.[203]

When the poor of Turin, Italy came to the Frassati home to pay their last respects to Blessed Pier Giorgio, they touched his hand or touched their rosaries to his hand. They had good reason.[204] Pier, who had ministered to the poor daily, *always* walked the streets of Turin with his rosary in hand, praying. It was like his trademark. And it made perfect sense. Just a few years earlier, when he was only seventeen, Pier had offered his entire life in a special consecration to the Blessed Mother. When we consecrate ourselves to Jesus through Mary, we are marked

---

[203] Sheen, *Treasure in Clay*, 187–199.

[204] The body part of a saint is a first-class relic. Items touched to a first-class relic become third-class relics. These grateful people touching their rosaries to Pier Giorgio's hand obviously recognized his sanctity.

as one of her own — spiritually branded. And there is no better ally on the road to Heaven.

Saint Maximilian Kolbe is known for his faithful devotion to the Blessed Virgin Mary. He joined in her mission to bring souls to Christ by forming an army under her leadership, the Militia Immaculata, whose members join with Mary in the spiritual battle against evil for the salvation of souls. The last section of the consecration prayer for members outlines the objective:

> Let me be a fit instrument in your immaculate and merciful hands for introducing and increasing your glory to the maximum in all the many strayed and indifferent souls, and thus help extend as far as possible the blessed kingdom of the most Sacred Heart of Jesus. For wherever you enter you obtain the grace of conversion and growth in holiness, since it is through your hands that all graces come to us from the most Sacred Heart of Jesus.[205]

Blessed Bartolo Longo helps us to understand that prayerfully meditating on the life of our Lord Jesus and His Blessed Mother Mary is transformational:

> Just as two friends, frequently in each other's company, tend to develop similar habits, so too, by holding familiar converse with Jesus and the Blessed Virgin, by meditating on the mysteries of the Rosary and by living the same life in Holy Communion, we can become, to the extent of our lowliness, similar to them and can learn from these

---

[205] Father Anselm Romb, *Total Consecration to Mary, Nine-Day Preparation in the Spirit of St. Maximilian Kolbe* (Libertyville, IL: Marytown Press, 2006), 94.

supreme models a life of humility, poverty, hiddenness, patience and perfection.[206]

The Holy Spirit works powerfully in the lives of the saints. They become "other Christs," members of His Mystical Body, the Church. Mary's mission, in cooperation with God, is to transform us into her Son, bringing new members into the Mystical Body of Christ. She continues to be irreplaceable in His redemptive work. Saint Louis de Montfort explains:

[The Holy Spirit] became fruitful through Mary whom he espoused. It was with her, in her and of her that He produced His masterpiece, God-made-man, and that he produces every day until the end of the world the members of the body of this adorable Head [producing members of the Body of Christ, the Church]. For this reason the more he [the Holy Spirit] finds Mary, his dear and inseparable spouse in a soul, the more powerful and effective he becomes in producing Jesus Christ in that soul and that soul in Jesus Christ.[207]

If we, like so many of the saints, want the Holy Spirit to work more profoundly in our lives, we will benefit tremendously by partnering with Mary, His Holy spouse. When it comes to following God's will, there is none better than Mary to guide us. And she comes highly recommended — by God Himself.[208]

---

[206] Brown, *Apostle of the Rosary*, 52.

[207] St. Louis de Montfort, *True Devotion to the Blessed Virgin* (Bay Shore, NY: Montfort Publications, 1993), 8.

[208] "When Jesus saw his mother, and the disciple whom he loved standing near, he said to his mother, 'Woman, behold, your son!' Then he said to the disciple, 'Behold, your mother!' And

Discover Your Next Mission from God

Our Mission from God

"God can use a good work, but He inhabits an anointed work."[209] There is an exponential characteristic to the work we do for the Lord when He calls us specifically to it. As with Saint Thérèse of Lisieux, it may remain hidden during our lives on earth. Or our mission, like Venerable Fulton Sheen's, might be one with celebrity status and fame. Regardless, God's will is perfectly suited to us. And when He *inhabits* that mission, it will bear fruit in ways we cannot conceive.

When pondering the lives of the saints, we see that they were devoted and obedient to the Church that Jesus established to carry out *His mission* on earth. Everything God asks of us, our special tasks, in one way or another, serve His primary mission — the salvation of souls. If we desire God's will, we need to follow Jesus' authority on earth: the one, holy, catholic, and apostolic Church. Staying true to the magisterial teachings of the Church is a great protection for us and in doing so, we demonstrate our trust in Jesus.

> He said to them, "But who do you say that I am?" Simon Peter replied, "You are the Christ, the Son of the living God." And Jesus answered him, "Blessed are you, Simon Bar-Jona! For flesh and blood has not revealed this to you, but my Father who is in heaven. And I tell you, you are Peter, and on this rock I will build my church, and the powers of death shall not prevail against it. I will give you the keys of the kingdom of heaven, and whatever you

---

from that hour the disciple took her to his own home" (John 19:26–27).

[209] A quote from the late Babsie Bleasdell from Trinidad.

bind on earth shall be bound in heaven, and whatever you loose on earth shall be loosed in heaven." (Matt. 16:15–19)

⌒

Reflection

The Blessed Virgin Mary's yes to God led her through beautiful joys, tremendous sorrows, and finally to exalted glories. She didn't know any of that when she gave her fiat, "Behold, I am the handmaid of the Lord; let it be to me according to your word" (Luke 1:38). But like our Blessed Mother's fiat, our yes to the Lord must be wholehearted, no matter where it leads.

We begin with the question, "Lord, what do you want me to do?" (CCC 2706). And we follow our Blessed Mother's instructions: "Do whatever He tells you" (John 2:5).

About the Author

Julie Onderko

Julie Onderko and her husband, Tom, reside in Milwaukie, Oregon, and are members of Christ the King Catholic Church. They have three grown sons and five grandchildren. Julie is the founder and president of the apostolate Catholic Finish Strong. She is a Catholic speaker and leads retreats and seminars. Currently she is enrolled in the Graduate School at the Augustine Institute to earn her Master of Arts in Theology. Julie can be contacted through her apostolate at www.CatholicFinishStrong. org.

Sophia Institute

Sophia Institute is a nonprofit institution that seeks to nurture the spiritual, moral, and cultural life of souls and to spread the Gospel of Christ in conformity with the authentic teachings of the Roman Catholic Church.

Sophia Institute Press fulfills this mission by offering translations, reprints, and new publications that afford readers a rich source of the enduring wisdom of mankind.

Sophia Institute also operates two popular online Catholic resources: CrisisMagazine.com and CatholicExchange.com.

Crisis Magazine provides insightful cultural analysis that arms readers with the arguments necessary for navigating the ideological and theological minefields of the day. *Catholic Exchange* provides world news from a Catholic perspective as well as daily devotionals and articles that will help you to grow in holiness and live a life consistent with the teachings of the Church.

In 2013, Sophia Institute launched Sophia Institute for Teachers to renew and rebuild Catholic culture through service to Catholic education. With the goal of nurturing the spiritual, moral, and cultural life of souls, and an abiding respect for the role and work of teachers, we strive to provide materials and programs that are at once enlightening to the mind and ennobling to the heart; faithful and complete, as well as useful and practical.

Sophia Institute gratefully recognizes the Solidarity Association for preserving and encouraging the growth of our apostolate over the course of many years. Without their generous and timely support, this book would not be in your hands.

www.SophiaInstitute.com
www.CatholicExchange.com
www.CrisisMagazine.com
www.SophiaInstituteforTeachers.org